4.00
set

GEORGE FREDERIC WATTS

VOL. I

THE ANNALS OF AN ARTIST'S LIFE

George Watts
Painted by his son, G. F. Watts, in 1835

GEORGE FREDERIC WATTS

VOLUME I

THE ANNALS OF AN ARTIST'S LIFE

BY

M. S. WATTS

HODDER & STOUGHTON
NEW YORK
GEORGE H. DORAN COMPANY

COPYRIGHT

ILLUSTRATIONS

FACE PAGE

George Watts. Painted by his Son, G. F. Watts, in 1835 *Frontispiece*

G. F. Watts, aged 17 (1835) 26

G. F. Watts. From a Photograph of a Drawing, now lost (1848) 106

The Countess Somers (1849) 122

G. F. Watts, by himself. A Portrait bequeathed by Sir William Bowman, Bart., to the National Gallery of British Art (1862–64) 218

Old Little Holland House. North-east aspect . . 159

Old Little Holland House. South-west aspect . . . 280

ERRATA

Page 61, line 4 from bottom, *for* villa *read* Villa.
 " 106, lines 14 and 15, *for* Cozens *read* Couzens.
 " 130, line 8, for *Chambers's Magazine* read *Chambers's Journal.*
 " 198, line 10, *for* Belgium *read* Belgian.
 " 204, line 19, *for* hoöked *read* hookĕd.
 " 241, line 24, *for* Gold-Hawk *read* Goldhawk.
 " 241 (footnote), *for* Mrs. Reginald Cholmondeley *read* Lady Alice Cholmondeley.
 " 244, line 5 from bottom, *for* Maddox *read* Madox.
 " 254, line 16, *for* Edward *read* Edwin.
 " 313, lines 3 and 7, *for* Evelene *read* Eveleen.
 " 319, line 16 from bottom, *for* Maddox *read* Madox.
 " 66, line 5, delete 2nd.

CHAPTER I

ALL that is most real and best in our lives is that which has no material reality—sentiment, love, honour, patriotism—these continue when the material things pass away.

G. F. WATTS.

CHAPTER I

Any record of the early life of George Frederic Watts now made, must certainly fail to give anything but a meagre account of his childhood, of his parents, or of the stock from which they came. No letters were preserved, and, as his life was a long one, those who knew him as a boy have long passed away; and now only do I seem to be conscious that the years when I had the privilege of being in close companionship with him were those of flower and fruit, and that, in my infinite contentment, these as it were habitually hid from my view any sight of the root and the stem.

His own opinion was that in these days too much is written of every one who comes at all before the public, and he envied, as I have heard Lord Tennyson say that he also envied, the oblivion that now hides every fact of the life of the man whose name stands first in literature.

He had a curious dislike to the sound of his surname, and habitually took trouble to avoid using it, a weakness best explained by his own simile: "One man may walk into a beautiful house with the dust of the highway on his boots, quite unconscious of this; while to another it would be so disagreeable as to amount to its being a real pain." He had fancies about the inheritance of a name, and used to say when he heard of one that pleased his ear, "Ah, if I had had a name such as that, I should have done my work better."

When Miss Thackeray, in her partly historical novel *Old Kensington*, skilfully touched in with words a miniature but most true and delicate portrait of him, she introduced him to her heroine as Mr. Royal: a name descriptive, in so far that the qualities of large generosity in all matters were essentially characteristic of him.

In answer to the question of a friend towards the middle of his life, he says: "You ask me in your letter if my name is British; I really know nothing about it. Being a lover of the beautiful, its want of music is distasteful to me; and for this reason, when I was younger, I often had serious thoughts of changing it, and should have done so if taking what did not belong to me had not seemed to be a very unsatisfactory alternative. I confess I should like to have a fine name and a great ancestry; it would have been delightful to me to feel as though a long line of worthies were looking down upon me and urging me to sustain their dignity. This I feel very strongly, all the time feeling still more strongly that to do good work in the world is a better thing than an accidental place in society. I like to see the good in all, and rather pride myself on being a real Liberal ; that is to say, being liberal enough to see and understand that there are and must be many conditions and many opinions."

He knew very little about his grandfathers or grandmothers in the flesh ; the subject of his ancestry did not interest him, nor could he believe that it would interest any one else. He never visited Hereford, where his grandfather lived and married Elizabeth Bradford in 1774, and died there early in the last century. He believed that he had Celtic blood in his veins, but knew of no proof of this. However, in the family of Elizabeth Bradford the Welsh names Edwards and Pugh occur, and he knew of the name Floris, as being common in the family as a Christian name ; but how it came there, or what nationality it represented, he did not know.

"I belong to a family that has gone down in the world," he said, referring to ties of blood relationship ; and the fact was painful to a nature so finely touched in all respects. In all humility he would turn with pleasure to the thought of a closer kinship he knew he might claim in aspiration and desire with great spirits of the past, and say, "I am a very poor relation, but of the family." His father was a man of fine perceptions, with some ambition ; one who was capable of guiding his son's self-education. On the mother's side, though she herself was of delicate constitution, he was fortunate in deriving something of the hardier fibre of the English yeoman. To that class her father and brother belonged, so probably from her were inherited qualities which tempered the nervous and æsthetic strain in her child.

This was all he knew of the family from which he came. There is a proverb in Gaelic of which a translation runs thus: "Behind the wave is the ocean," and big events lay behind the years into which George Frederic Watts and his generation of brother-artists were born. When reviewing progress in the eighteenth century, Mr. Lecky wrote: "Few questions in history are more perplexing and perhaps more insoluble than the causes which govern the great manifestations of æsthetic genius." Without attempting to discuss such a problem, it can be affirmed without fear of contradiction that English art, already great in portraiture and in landscape, received a new impulse from the men whose births occurred now and in the following years. They appeared as a group, and seemed to be sons of their age more than of any particular family, the results, as it were, of some common aspiration. Perhaps the victory of Waterloo had relieved a tension caused by a long series of wars, and men to carry forward the arts of peace were needed. The story of one of these does, I venture to think, show that in his regard for the honour of his country he was not unworthy of the heroes who won Waterloo.

Towards the end of life he wrote: "My great and ever constant desire is to identify artistic outcome with all that is good and great in every creed and utterance, and all that is inspiring in every record of heroism, of suffering, of effort, and of achievement." This desire had inspired him from the very beginning of his working life.

Some time towards the end of the eighteenth century George Watts, the father, left his father's workshop in Hereford, where, as I was told by a granddaughter, they made musical instruments, though his son writes of him as a cabinet-maker. He came to London, and in 1818 describes himself as a pianoforte manufacturer. But the ambition of invention filled his thoughts, and its dazzle was always before his eyes, leading him into desultory experiments and neglect of more practical work ; and it is probable that failure of business and other troubles had already beset his steps when, in 1816, he married, as his second wife, Harriet, daughter of Frederic Smith, herself a widow. To them, living in a house in Queen Street, Bryanston Square, the father being already in his forty-fourth year and the mother in her thirty-first, their eldest son was born, as the entry in the Prayer Book carefully records, at one o'clock on Sunday morning, the 23rd of February 1817. They christened him George after his father and grandfather, and Frederic after a brother of his mother to whom she was much attached. There was a private baptism, and the godfather who was present was given the little basin that served as font, and this with its ewer was carefully preserved by him.

The children of George Watts's first marriage

were three—a boy at this time aged sixteen, and two girls of fifteen and thirteen years old; and though the second marriage brought some addition to the slender purse, it was probably quite put out of account by Mrs. Watts's invalid condition, which greatly added to the cares and anxieties of the home.

Of this marriage four sons were born in quick succession, but the youngest survived his birth only for a few weeks, and the two others did not live much beyond infancy; for in the winter of 1823 the little boys all fell ill from an unusually severe outbreak of measles. The parents' concern at first was chiefly for their eldest, George Frederic, but that thread of life, fragile as it was, proved to be stronger than they knew; and he lived, while both his little brothers died and within the space of a few days were buried in one grave. With so much strain upon the delicate constitution of his mother, it is easy to understand why her image remained to the last in her son's memory as one entirely connected with sadness. He remembered her chiefly when passing with the sad slow steps that mark the progress of consumption to her grave by her little sons, where in 1826 she was laid; a lovable, patient, and good woman, of whom her stepdaughters always spoke in admiration. There is no picture of her, but a photograph taken in old age of her sister shows that, though George must have greatly resembled his father, the slight frame and delicate poise of the small head—and I believe his brown eyes—are all characteristic of the family of his mother.

The father was now for the second time a widower, and his two grown-up daughters continued to take charge of the home, as they had already done for some years. These four completed the home circle.

The son's portrait of his father, painted about the year 1836 and reproduced as a frontispiece to this book, discloses the characteristics of a man delicately minded, full of aspiration if not strong of purpose. This, as his son described him, he was. The pathos of the eyes seems to show that he knew that the aim of his own life had not been attained; in the mouth there is something of petulant protest against circumstances that had proved too hard for his overcoming; and yet, underlying all, there is in the expression of the eyes a hope—perhaps a confident hope for another; as if he saw the light that was rising for him in the day of his grey hairs.

In an old desk once his, which since my husband's death has come into my possession, there lies a little agate seal, upon which may be seen very unskilfully engraved, evidently by no professional hand, the symbol of a rising sun. Knowing that the father's inventive turn of mind led him to lose time by taking up too many arts and crafts, it may not be too fanciful to suggest that this attempt at engraving was by his own hand, and that the little seal bears in its device something very personal connected with this hope of his later years—the son whom he had certainly "set as a seal upon his heart."

He had some taste for art; even as a young man at Hereford he cared to buy good engravings, an etching by Rembrandt and a few by Greuze being amongst the still existing possessions of that date. He used both brush and pencil, though he was never proficient, and as none of these attempts remain, evidently never satisfied himself in this direction; on the other hand, he carefully dated and kept many of his son's earliest original drawings, and also preserved some of the engravings from which the little fellow's very exact copies were made. He either inherited or collected a few books, in good editions, the only luxury of the home; for instance, *Lestrange's Fables*, some plays of the time of Charles II., *The Seven Champions of Christendom*, and others, the disappearance of which was a matter of regret to his son. After the death of his wife, his chief concern was for little George. "His father watched him at every turn," were the expressive words of one who remembered his boyhood; remembering also with a tender clearness, though looking down the dim distance of seventy years, that his playmates looked eagerly for little George's coming to join in their games, adding that she could well remember the pleasure of hearing his light step running to find them at play.

It is good to know there were fields still in that part of London, fields rich with buttercups and wild flowers; and that there the little George played. He could remember a day when, after roaming about on a bit of ground where timber was being cleared, he sat down at one end of a fallen tree, when an impressive figure in a long black cloak came slowly up and seated himself silently at the other end. The man with the fine thoughtful face that so attracted the boy's attention was Edward Irving.

A few rare visits were paid to his godfather's farm in Sussex, and thus he made acquaintance with country pleasures, but on the whole the memory of his boyhood was not a happy one, chiefly because ill-health made him unable to enjoy what boys of his age were enjoying. Neither was he able to give himself to consecutive study such as his eager mind desired.

Amongst his earliest drawings there is one—whether an original or a copy he could not recollect. It is undated, but in a round childish hand the name of "Sisyphus" is written; and comparing these pot-hooks with his handwriting at ten years old, a time when copies made by him could not as facsimiles be bettered, it is safe to conclude that the Sisyphus belongs to some years earlier—probably to the age of six or seven. With firm and rather black strokes of the pencil the strong muscles of the condemned one are very descriptively given, and there is pathos in the choice of this subject by a child who indeed knew too early the steepness of the way of life and the burden of its anxieties.

GEORGE FREDERIC WATTS

It has been suggested to me by a physician that the attacks of headache, with vertigo and sickness, from which he suffered so continually may have been due to eye-strain. With a highly nervous temperament (not sufficiently well understood) perhaps also these were due to the strain of being called upon when too young to share his father's disappointments and anxieties. No doubt these trials would have, on the elders of the family, the effect of producing a tendency to irritability, by laying nerves bare to the slightest annoyance, and although little George was well loved by father and sisters, they were probably unaware of the torment he suffered from the constant dread of recurring outbursts of temper. In retrospect he concluded that the nervousness of his later life was greatly due to the anxiety he suffered in those early days, when these thunderstorms of passion were continually brewing and at any moment likely to burst upon the household. In speaking of this it was characteristic of him to blame no particular member of the family, and indeed he appeared to take pains not to mention any name. The attacks of headache, from which he suffered so acutely all through his boyhood, averaged, he believed, something like one in every week, and they would prostrate him completely for two days. At the best of times he was conscious of a *malaise* which seemed to halve all his pleasures; but when recovering from the worse, the better would seem by comparison almost bliss, and he would lie quietly enjoying the sense of freedom from actual pain, when a strange mystic sensation would come over him, as if his feet had travelled off on some wonderful journey through space; further and infinitely further they went, and it gave him a strange sort of joy to seem to follow, and yet stay behind. He often alluded to this, and wondered what explanation there might be to account for the repetition of a sensation so fantastic, and yet to him so real.

During the hours of enforced quiet he made a little friend that became very dear to him. He tamed a sparrow so completely that it perched on his head as he lay in bed, ate from his plate, and was a cheerful and much beloved companion. Tragedy of course overtook it in the end, and the grief he felt when he saw it drop dead at his feet was not forgotten. "I feel the sorrow as keenly to-day as if it happened yesterday," he said. The end was the more terrible as it was brought about by his own hand; in shutting up his sparrow for the night he accidentally caught in the doorway the little head which, unnoticed by him, popped out for another last word.

In those days he looked very young for his age, and, according to his own account, was so backward that he was filled with shame as each birthday came round; but, if the boy may be judged by the man, he took his measure by the standard of what he wished to attain rather than by that of other boys of his own age. "Self-confidence," he said, "is called a fault of youth, but if that is so, I think I may say it was one which I had not ; I only knew one thing, which was that I knew nothing."

His health preventing him from attending, with any sort of regularity, any classes or school, he was taught, or taught himself as best he could, at home. He learnt to read fairly early, his father giving a good direction to his boy's choice of books. Later in life he could not hear without something like indignation of boys who were indifferent to and wasteful of advantages which had been withheld from him; perhaps above all that of robust health. But Poverty may also bring her gift of compensation; want of means made the books few, yet, as they were choice, the limitation had this advantage that he read them over and over again till they became a part of his world and of his being. Without the imposition of dreary tasks of grammar, he entered freely and of his own choice into the Greek mind, through such translations as were accessible to him. The *Iliad*, perhaps the first and best beloved of all, he read and re-read until gods and heroes were his friends and acquaintances; he thought of them as such, judged critically of their words and actions, and was deeply moved by all that was noble and beautiful and restrained ; he knew this to be a very living school, and every fibre of his being answered to the splendour of the great epic. And so, while ill-health held him back from all pleasures of the more active sort, there was given instead this leisure, in which his imaginative mind could roam the windy plains of Troy, or climb the heights of Olympus. Moving through the dim light of a London atmosphere, in his dull little room he saw " the bright-eyed Athene in the midst bearing the holy ægis, that knoweth neither age nor death," and dreamed that he too might be an ægis-bearer of that which cannot grow old, the utterance of the human mind in the language of an art.

Very early in life he also drew upon that treasure-house of healthy and splendid romance, the novels of Sir Walter Scott, whose knights and cavaliers often supplied subjects for his pencil, and with the Greek heroes inspired his earliest compositions. These novels inspired him then, and throughout life, and were—with the novels of Miss Austen—the books that he turned to most often when tired or unwell.

His family were members of the Anglican Church, and into that Church he had been baptized; but the point of view held in the home was too limited; a narrow Sabbatarian habit made Sunday a burden to his young mind, and there was no help for the little fellow in the bare and dreary Church services to which he was taken. A preacher in a black gown spoke of wrath to come, and his reason and his æsthetic instincts were shocked, so much so that he remembered that at that time he thoroughly believed all religious teachers to be insincere.

He sometimes spoke with surprise of the independent view he remembered to have taken quite early in life. "While I felt," he said, "for the subject of religion so great a reverence that it was difficult for me to speak about it, I reasoned and rebelled against the unreality of ordinary religious teaching." The early religious bent of his mind, through the teaching then received, might have been towards the narrowest side of the Evangelical school; for instance, on Sundays he was never allowed to read anything but a so-called religious book; on this day a newspaper was absolutely forbidden, and all books except Bunyan's *Pilgrim's Progress* and the Bible and Prayer Book were put away.

The pictures in the Bible and in the Queen Anne Prayer Book (in which the entry of the day and hour of his birth is made so exactly) must have somewhat consoled him, until he had made copies of the illustrations so many times that at last he exhausted their fascinations. In one of these the eye of the Deity is given—a realistic eye, large in the sky—from which a ray of light, solid as metal, streams upon the head of Guy Fawkes, who with his lantern is going about his evil business.

He remembered with what a revulsion of feeling he heard as a little boy the story told of some man who during the week had neglected to read his Bible, but being sorry for this on Sunday, was in the act of taking it down from the shelf where it had lain, when he was suddenly struck dead as a just retribution for his sin. The horror he then felt at such a conception of divine justice he could not forget. He had in fact realised, when quite young, a certain want of correspondence between his own nature and his surroundings.

Yet one result of the early home training was that he knew the Bible well, and remembered every detail of the Old Testament stories, and, as he retold these, just by an accent here and there he would throw new and original comment upon them, quite his own. Very possibly the element of Puritanical austerity, which made Sunday so dreary to the little boy, as it did not narrow his views nor make him pretend to a piety he did not feel, was valuable as a discipline; and to this may have been due a power of self-control which in so highly nervous and emotional a temperament was certainly remarkable.

Of the purpose he set before himself when beginning to study art he once said to me: "From the very first I determined to do the very best possible to me; I did not hope to make a name, or think much about climbing to the top of the tree, I merely set myself to do the utmost I could, and I think I may say I have never relaxed; to this steady endeavour I owe everything. Hard work, and keeping the definite object of my life in view, has given me whatever position I now have. And I may add, what I think is an encouragement to others, that very few have begun life with fewer advantages, either of health, wealth, or position, or any exceptional intellect. Any success I may have had is due entirely to steadiness of purpose."

He could not recall any time from his earliest childhood when he did not use a pencil; and he seems from the first to have taken such pains with his work that it might be assumed this faculty was inherited. A comparison of his copies in chalk, set beside the original etching on copper with a metal point, prove with what extreme care the boy of eleven or twelve years old counted and copied every line, sharpening the chalk, as he well remembered, between every three or four strokes. This faculty for taking pains, together with an enthusiasm for his work, made anything like the ordinary training of an art student quite unnecessary. His own axiom that in art there was "everything to be learnt, and very little to be taught," was spoken out of his own experience. It may have been that in later years, when giving advice to students, he never quite realised the value of an opportunity afforded for exclusive devotion to its study within the walls of a School of Art. The limitations of a boyhood precluded by ill-health from the usual games, and a temperament that to some extent marked him out for solitary study, may possibly have made it difficult for him to understand the advantage which schools offer to others more exposed to the temptations of the active and social life. The advice given by him may at times have been misunderstood; it certainly was if it was taken to mean that he held that art did not demand arduous and exclusive study for many years; a study which in one sense must never cease; the early training he held was merely to find out how to study. He wished the student to understand that he must not depend upon academic rules, and very little upon the experience of a teacher : all that others could give him was quite elementary; for the right development of the best that was in him he had to equip himself by an intelligent study of the book of nature and in the traditions of great art.

As a consequence of bad health, regularity of work in boyhood was not possible, but a fortunate circumstance gave him an opportunity which otherwise could not have been his. His father, in his work of pianoforte making, happened to be associated with a Hanoverian of the name of Behnes, who had married in England and had three sons. The Behnes family had at one time living in the same house with themselves an old Frenchman, a sculptor by profession in England, but quite probably a refugee of the French *noblesse*; and his influence caused both Henry and William Behnes to take up the profession of art. Henry died early in Rome, but William, though already helping his father in his work, gave it up for the study of art, and became for a time one of the most successful and popular sculptors of portrait medallions and busts then living. He made the first portrait bust of the little Princess Victoria, and on her coming to the throne was appointed by her "Sculptor in Ordinary to Her Majesty."

His first studio was in Dean Street, Soho, and here little George, then not more than ten years old, went in and out as he liked. In his recollection the best work accomplished by William Behnes was in pencil. More especially he recalled one magnificent drawing from the antique group of Arria and Pætus, and he often regretted that these were lost, and that falling into ignorant hands, they had in all probability been destroyed. Henry Weekes, the sculptor, mentions Behnes's paintings upon vellum as being the finest he had ever seen. Writing of him, he says, "The genius of Behnes was a sort of Mephistopheles, always at his side allowing him always to fancy he was going to be pleased, yet eventually leading him to destruction."

But it was Charles Behnes, the brother, an invalid and malformed, of whom but slight mention is made in any account of the sculptor, to whom George became attached. Some time early in the 'thirties William Behnes removed to the studio (then No. 13 Osnaburgh Street) afterwards tenanted by Mr. Foley, and where Sir Frederic Leighton modelled his athlete, the present occupant being Mr. Brock. It was of this studio that my husband most often spoke. William and his brother Charles seemed to have had a full appreciation of his gifts; and as Charles was some twenty years older, the contact with his maturer mind was of great value to him. Charles was an intellectual man, and this his brother the sculptor was not. His liberal view of life, and understanding of the best things in literature, and above all his goodness, attracted George to him. As was his habit at all times, it so happened that in speaking of these early friends he never emphasised the fact that in this respect William Behnes contrasted badly with his brother; and that indeed in William the moral sense was absent; he would merely say that William had no strength of character, and that while Charles lived he kept his brother's business affairs in order, and held him up from moral slips as far as he was able; but that after Charles died—somewhere about 1844—William "went all to pieces," as he expressed it. It seems, however, certain, from what is known of the story otherwise, that thus early in life the boy stood between a good and an evil influence, and that he chose the good. It was during these early days that a friend of Charles Behnes, a miniature painter, gave him his first lesson in the use of oil-colour, lent him a painting by Sir Peter Lely to copy, and at the same time gave him a simple practical formula for the colours to be used. This copy, full of the characteristics of Lely's work, is now placed with a small collection of early works in the Watts Collection at Compton in Surrey.[1]

[1] Throughout this book, for the sake of brevity, the name Compton Gallery is used, but as there are more than twenty towns or villages of that name, it must be understood that this Compton is in Surrey, equally distant from Guildford and Godalming (three miles).

GEORGE FREDERIC WATTS

About this date his father took some of his son's drawings to the President of the Royal Academy, Sir Martin Archer Shee, and being anxious to know if it was right to encourage his son to be an artist, asked his opinion upon them. The verdict, given after looking at the drawings, was, "I can see no reason why your son should take up the profession of art." The father, however, was undaunted and allowed the boy to have his way.

One can fancy the light figure moving about the big studio, using up every atom of daylight, and probably singing at his work ; a habit never wholly given up if work was going to his mind. He had sung from his childhood, and well remembered his regret when the inevitable change came and the quality of voice peculiar to boyhood was lost.

Even when he was working at home, he often went to Osnaburgh Street, and sat there whilst the studio grew dark, talking of many things with Charles Behnes. Early in life he had made acquaintance with some elementary books on science recommended to him by his friend ; they discussed Shakespeare, Virgil, Ossian, and many another author. He had some fun too with his mentors, once having amused himself by painting a fraudulent Van Dyck on purpose to see if they would be deceived. The head was painted from himself, the dress being of course of the time of Charles I. When the surface was hard enough, he poked his picture up the chimney, and waited till it had sufficiently mellowed; he then took it round to the studio, where, with some pretence of hesitation, he suggested that he thought he had discovered a Van Dyck. The sculptor looked at it critically, and then said: "Well, I would not venture to say that it is by Van Dyck, but it certainly is by no mean hand." When the trick was confessed, Behnes angrily cried out, "Why the deuce don't you always paint like that?" It was probably about this time that Benjamin Haydon—amongst English artists the discoverer of the true worth of the Elgin Marbles—one day noticed a sketch-book in the hand of a boy who passed him in the street; possibly also he may have noticed something unusual in the face of one setting out on his quest to find the true and the beautiful: anyhow he laid his hand kindly upon young Watts's shoulder, and said, "May a fellow-student look at your work?" He spoke encouragingly, and invited the boy to his studio, but for some reason, probably owing to a certain hesitation in putting himself forward, he never went; and this was their only meeting.

After Mrs. Watts's death the family had removed from Queen Street to Star Street, Marylebone, probably for the sake of greater economy, and it was in this house, I believe, that a room was set apart as the studio; but his first studio (built as such) was in Roberts Road, Hampstead Road, where it stood in the garden at the back of the house.

GEORGE FREDERIC WATTS

Talking once of early rising, it was mentioned that it was far more difficult to get up early when young than later in life; and his answer was, "Don't I know that very well, for I could only overcome the difficulty myself by not going to bed at all: I used not to undress, but rolled myself in a thick dressing-gown, and lay on the floor of my studio, sometimes on two chairs, until I had taught myself to awake and get up with the sun." The habit once acquired was never lost. In his eighty-eighth year, as soon as daylight permitted he rose and set to work. If he was ill and obliged to remain in bed, he would generally ask to have the curtains and blinds closed, once explaining, "I cannot bear it, the light calls to me."

In his early days the fight against self had to be continually maintained, and taking into account the ever-recurrent interruptions from illness, the fact that he never allowed himself to become desultory in his work shows that the character was resolute then as it remained unaltered to the end.

Up to this time, having carefully studied from anatomical casts, and still more assiduously from the skeleton, a knowledge of which, as the foundation of all good drawing, he placed first in importance, his pencil had been busy from childhood with original designs of the gods, kings, knights, and ladies that peopled his brain at the time; and before he was sixteen he had begun to undertake small commissions for portraits, drawn sometimes in coloured chalk, sometimes in pencil, for which he asked the sum of five shillings.

Affairs at home had been going from bad to worse. The father, becoming more desultory, gave elementary lessons in music, tuned pianos, and did any clerical work that came in his way. His son was glad to think that after the age of sixteen he never cost his father anything, and that later he was able to support him till his death in 1845. By the year 1835 the young student's power of accomplishment was maturing fast, but, to perfect himself further, he made up his mind to enter the schools of the Royal Academy.

The ivory disc for a student's admission is still extant with the name and date engraved upon it: "George Frederic Watts, Admitted April 30th, 1835," and on the reverse, "Royal Academy Antique School." His name also appears upon the books during the two following years, but at that time the schools were practically closed for half the year, the space being so limited that the rooms were required when Exhibitions were being held. The teaching at that time was exceedingly disappointing; as he said himself, a few years later, "there was no teaching at all": he therefore attended the School only long enough to satisfy himself that he could learn quite as much in his own studio. "There was no test," he said, "no examination of the pupils"—in a word, an absolute want of instruction; and when speaking of this time he would say that he learnt in no school save one, that of Pheidias, and in that school he had never ceased to learn.

In 1835 the President was Sir Martin Archer Shee, and the Keeper Mr. William Hilton, who had but recently lost his wife—the sister of the painter Peter de Wint—a blow which he felt so severely that it undermined his health, and is said to have shortened his life. Outwardly he was an austere man of few words, one from whom praise was worth winning. It was therefore no small matter when this was gained.

It so happened that twice during this time at the Academy Schools young Watts's drawings were picked out both by Mr. Hilton and by his fellow-students as being certain of a medal; the first time for a drawing from the antique, the second for a drawing from the life. He remembered it as a thing of yesterday, and described it thus:

"When the result of the judging was known, and that my drawing had not been given the medal, I was much pleased by Hilton's coming across the room to me and whispering, 'Never mind, you ought to have had it'; I liked that better than the medal."

Another day Mr. Hilton pointed to the drawing on George Watts's easel, and speaking generally to the students, said, "That is the way I like to see a drawing done." The praise was remembered.

G. F. Watts
aged seventeen

GEORGE FREDERIC WATTS

He had, however, so far formed his own opinion upon the course of practice he believed would best develop and strengthen his powers that he recollected taking a small picture he had painted of a dying knight to show to Mr. Hilton, who commended it, but at the same time told him on no account to attempt anything original in the way of composition. He weighed the advice, believed it to be mistaken, and went on with his imaginative work. "I was right, I believe, and Hilton wrong. Although he was right in warning me against drifting into mere picture making, he should have said, 'Do this kind of thing certainly, but take care that you make very careful studies from nature as well.'"

The year 1837 found him hard at work in his own studio, this being a room in Clipston Street; and in March of that year he sent in to the Academy for exhibition the picture called the "Wounded Heron," painted from the dead bird he happened to see in a poulterer's shop. Struck by its beauty, he bought it, and worked from it as rapidly as the conditions required, but with the utmost care and painstaking.

It is impossible not to see in the pathos of the outstretched wing something more than a prophecy of the pathos in the wing of Love defending the door of Life of forty years later—young Love impotent against the inevitable—much also of the same mind, taking note of the mysteries in the drama of life suggested by the falcon high in the blue over the dying heron—

one beautiful child of nature joyfully pursuing another to the death, and the mounted falconer also following gaily, and possessed with the joy of the chase.

This picture [1] was given a place upon the walls of the Academy that year, when he also exhibited two portraits, each under the title of "The Portrait of a Young Lady." For one of these, a portrait of little Miss Hopkins, the delicate sketch in chalk now lies in a scrap-book of early drawings; he painted her three times, and one of these portraits hangs amongst other early works in the Compton Gallery.

It was about this time that an acquaintance began between him and Mr. Nicholas Wanostrocht—an Englishman by birth, though Belgian by descent. He inherited, so to speak, a school from his grandfather and uncle, where education was carried on upon very original lines; but to the world his name is best known as Nicholas Felix the cricketer, the author of *Felix on the Bat*. It was with some idea of having illustrations made of the various positions of the cricketer, as the game at that time was played, that he commissioned George Watts to make the series of seven such positions—afterwards drawn by him upon stone. Four of these are portraits of Felix himself, the others of Fuller Pilch and of Alfred

---

[1] "The Wounded Heron" was returned to him in 1888. One Sunday, talking with Mrs. Henry Holiday of his early work, he spoke of it as his first picture at the Royal Academy, and regretted that it was lost. Mrs. Holiday suggested that I should advertise. By a strange coincidence a letter from the possessor, a dealer in Newcastle, was already in the post offering the picture to us for a small sum.

Mynn. Five of the original drawings, still in his possession in 1895, he offered to Lord Harris, the President of the Marylebone Cricket Club, where they are now placed.

An amusing incident brought about this gift. A friend paying a visit in a country house in Cornwall, on going upstairs with his host one night on their way to bed, paused with his lighted candle before a lithograph of a cricketer hanging on the staircase wall, and said at a venture, " Only Watts could have drawn that leg." This led to enquiries, proving that the guess was right, and my husband, finding that the original drawings would be of value to the Marylebone Cricket Club, accordingly offered them.

Nicholas Wanostrocht and he found much pleasure in each other's society, and the evenings spent at Alfred House, Blackheath, were amongst the happiest of the recollections of this time. Mr. Wanostrocht was a very talented man, and his school was for some time very successful. One opinion, which he was able to demonstrate in a practical manner, was that every boy, with talent or without, was capable on Hullah's system of being taught to sing. The music master at the school of the name of May was an assistant of Hullah's, and on this (the Do, re, mi) system he taught, and every pupil of the school, and every member of the family as well, could sing and read from sight. Sometimes in later years, when listening to even very excellent singing by choristers, my husband would say, "They do not sing as well as Wanostrocht's boys used to sing." These were happy evenings for him, and for others too. In a letter from an acquaintance of that time, she says, " I am glad to find you remember the happy old times spent at Blackheath ; I think they were to many of us happier than any of our later years."

Another correspondent recalls the whole holiday given to the boys—of whom he had been one—in 1843, "in honour of the successful cartoon by the rising genius of whom Wanostrocht was an early and enthusiastic appreciator." It was now that George cultivated his voice with some care, studied French and Italian, and worked at Greek also; but the regret of his life was that the time which necessarily had to be given to his art left but too small a margin for such serious work, and he was therefore never able to read Homer in the original with pleasure.

A trifle, perhaps, but one which shows the earnestness of the young mind, is to be found in a little copy of the book *Il Pastor Fido*, where in pencil, the writing being still somewhat unformed, is scribbled on one page, G. F. Watts, and under the name, " *qui ne le sait lire, qu'il est malheureux !* "— to which there is an addition, probably made later, " Il libro di G. F. Watts," and these words follow in Italian : " It seems to me that I have a way made for me, and that no one could have a better opportunity for hoping to achieve something. If I can, I shall feel well paid for all the past." The day he wrote those words there must have been a rift in the clouds : on others, when he painted a small picture — somewhat earlier than 1837 as he believed — the clouds must have been lying very thick and low upon him. In this the kneeling figure seems to be a bit of history, part of the young painter's own experience. It was not his intention to represent "The Man of Sorrows" — it is but the figure of one of the many human souls who have gone along the Via Crucis. The impression given out from that picture is of loneliness and bareness; the background represents night, and the grey streak on the horizon that the sun has long gone down. The thin vesture, with few folds and little colour, hangs severely about the spare young figure, who with closed eyes and bowed head has fallen upon his knees as if the burden of the day had been too great for him. Now withdrawn into self, wearied but tranquil, an inward vision is being revealed, in token of which a silvery shaft of light is falling down upon him; and round his head the ring of a golden Glory begins to form.

Much of this early time of life was not happy, and the remembrance was so fraught with pain that those who loved him did not care to recall it to his mind, by asking questions which can never now be answered. In the face of ill-health, and with the additional burden laid on him by the necessity for earning money, the difficulties must have been great; for the boy determined to pursue a general course of education as well as the study and practice of his art. He was much attached to his father, the failure of whose life was a great pain to him; and there was much of hardship in those years to jar upon both of those finely touched natures, for the father was a man of peculiar refinement of mind, and I have been told of manner also.

About this time George Watts made his first acquaintance with the Greek family of Ionides, a friendship which during his long life descended from generation to generation. The first of the family to come into touch with the young painter was Constantine Ionides, the head of a Greek Merchant House in London, with branches in Constantinople and Athens. In a letter of a later date Mr. Ionides recalls his first visit to young Watts's studio:

"I recollect as if it was yesterday my visit with Mr. E. Riley to see a portrait of a little girl that you were painting when he recommended you for copying Lane's portrait of my father. Equally well your first visit to my office, when you brought both original and copy, and I said at once to Mr. G. F. Cavafy, who was present, that I preferred by far the copy, and that I was going to keep the copy and send the original to Constantinople. This was in the early spring of 1837. That Cavafy was quite startled at the novelty of my preferring a work for which I had paid £10 to one that cost £63, and seemed quite incredulous, when suddenly in the outer office I heard the voice of Du Roveray, who was considered a good connoisseur, and was occasionally employed by the Rothschilds to value pictures for them—when I called him, and he at once confirmed my view."

On being asked to point out the original, Du Roveray replied, "I cannot tell you that, but I can tell you which is by far the best painting of the two."

From that time onwards George Watts had many Greek friends, Mr. Constantine Ionides being the first and, at that time, the most affluent and generous. He spoke also with pleasure of kind friends of the name of Ellis, who had a charming house in West End Lane, in which he made a water-colour study of some groups of fine trees. Of these friends he writes in later years, "Amongst the many changes in my life, which I should be ungrateful to call unsuccessful, I constantly recall the pleasant time spent at West End Lane : seldom could enjoyment be more real, or leave less to regret."

At this house he was introduced to Mr. Roebuck, who sat to him for a portrait, also engraved by the artist on stone, and gave him the singular commission to paint a portrait of Jeremy Bentham from the effigy which had been modelled in wax as the terms of Bentham's Will directed. The picture George Watts then painted was once exhibited with his name, and with no further explanation ; upon which he wrote as follows to the secretary of the exhibition :

"As a portrait honestly painted from life

becomes one of the most valuable of records, it is important that the spurious and the faithful representation should not be confounded. I therefore beg to state that the portrait of Jeremy Bentham, to which my name is affixed, is not from life, but was painted by me, then a mere lad, from a wax figure which was so far curious that it covered, I believe, the philosopher's bones, and was dressed in his clothes."

Besides the portrait of his father already mentioned, there are a few portraits in oil colour of small size belonging to the year 1836—that is the earliest date I know of for accomplished work in this medium—one of Mr. Richard Edmonds, of Mr. Richard Jarvis, and in 1837–38 of the Rev. Alfred Oliver Wellsted. Two portraits (on one canvas) of Miss Alice Spring Rice were, I think, painted before 1839. Friends of the name of Jarvis gave him many of his earliest commissions, both for portraits and subject pictures. In one of these, a hunting scene, the slight figure of a boy holding the bridle of his horse was painted from himself, and from this I gather that when more than twenty years old he looked very young; one might take the figure to have been drawn from a lad of sixteen. Some time before he left Italy he had painted the three children of the Earl of Gainsborough, several portraits of the family of Admiral Hamilton, Miss Brunton, Miss Jardine, Madame Ionides, Miss Galenga, and the group of the Ionides family, this being as to scale the most important undertaking of this time, though not by any means his first commission as some writers have said. Mr. Haskett-Smith, an old friend of the Hamilton family, told me that Captain Hamilton (as he then was) was so much pleased with the work done for him by the young painter that instead of the £20 named as the price, he sent £25. " But," Mr. Haskett-Smith continued, " Mr. Watts immediately insisted on painting the portrait of the baby, which he threw in ! "

He went into Derbyshire to paint or draw portraits for a Derbyshire squire, Mr. Offley Shore ; and later again to the same neighbourhood to paint the children of a Mr. Bagshaw ; but, though the commissions for portraits formed of necessity a great part of his work, he had already determined to make portraiture subordinate to creative work, notwithstanding that he was advised by painters much older than himself to wait till his later years, when his fortune would be sufficient to allow him to indulge in the luxury of composition. But he kept his own counsel, and went on his way, learning later that one at least of his advisers had lived to acknowledge that he had been wrong, and that when in affluent days he would have turned to the use of that gift, it had perished.

Among other acquaintances of this time was one with a young man whose early death some years later he ever believed to be a serious loss to the world. George Watts was painting the portrait of the lad's father, a man who had had some success in business. Though the family were not altogether congenial to him, the mother being a vain and foolish woman, on one occasion when he was invited to dine and spend the evening, he accepted. When he rose to go, rather to his annoyance, the son of the house, then a lad of about fifteen or sixteen years old, whom he knew to be leading a very fast life, got up also, and offered to walk across the park with him. And so it was that, under the dome of a sky brilliant with stars, the two pacing along together came to talk of many things, when suddenly some word that was said caused the younger of the two to open his heart and to make confession of his life. Plunged from his earliest days by a dissolute father into vicious company and vicious ways, something now stirred within him to make him realise the misery of it all. They were but as "ships that pass in the night," and did not cross each other's way again for several years, four of which George had spent in Italy.

When they met again in the studio of Behnes, the boy had grown to manhood; tall and handsome—a brilliant talker and a delightful companion. He was deep in the study of some branch of science—at one of the Universities, I think; his professors predicting for him a very distinguished career, but this promise was unhappily ended by an early death. When they were alone he confided to George that he dated the whole change in his life from the night when they had walked together across the park.

When I asked what had been said, I remember the answer was simply, "We talked of the stars."

CHAPTER II

It is not only for the moment that the artist works. In common with all who enrich the world his work will come to be regarded for what it is, not with reference to the period of its production. Two thousand years hence, whether a picture was painted in the sixteenth century and in Italy, or in the nineteenth in England, will not matter. It will be common property to all who care for art.

G. F. WATTS.

CHAPTER II

"THE Commissioners appointed by the Queen for the purpose of enquiring whether on the rebuilding of Her Majesty's palace of Westminster wherein her Parliament is wont to assemble, advantage might not be taken of the opportunity thereby afforded of promoting and encouraging the Fine Arts in the United Kingdom," issued on April 25, 1842, notice of a competition in cartoons, in size not less than 10 and not more than 15 feet in their longest dimensions, to be made in chalk or charcoal, without colour, the figures not less than life size, the subject to be from English history, from Spenser, Shakespeare, or Milton. The finished drawings were to be sent in the first week of May 1843, but subsequently this time was extended to the first week in June. There were 140 cartoons in the Exhibition opened at the Westminster Hall in that month. They all bore only a mark on the back, which tallied with a mark on the sealed letter containing the artist's name and address. The prizes offered were three of £300, three of £200, and five of £100 each.

GEORGE FREDERIC WATTS

In a volume of Parliamentary reports labelled 'Fine Arts' the award of the premium of £300 each stands thus in order:

"Cæsar's First Invasion of Britain," Edward Armitage.

"Caractacus led in Triumph through the Streets of Rome," George Frederic Watts.

"The First Trial by Jury," Charles West Cope.

The volume of reports was sent to my husband in 1902 by a stranger to him,[1] who had the kindly thought to bestow it because of a pencilled note written on the margin of the catalogue of the cartoons which it contains. Against the "Caractacus led in Triumph through the Streets of Rome" the note in a delicate handwriting runs thus: "Leaves nothing to be wished, in my opinion should stand number one."

That one of the three chief premiums had fallen to his lot came as a complete surprise to George Watts. Young as he was he had schooled himself to be very temperate in any forecast of success for himself. Young Horsley first told him that he had heard it rumoured that he was one of the winners of the first prizes, but he assured Horsley that this was quite impossible, as he had very much doubted whether it was worthy of being entered at all.

The fact was that in the endeavour to fix the drawing by some process of steaming, the clumsy

[1] Edwin Seward, F.R.I.B.A.

method that was then the only one known, he had, as he believed, entirely ruined it, and had turned it with its face to the wall and taken up other work. A morning or two before the last day for sending in he looked at it once more, and finding it not altogether hopeless, he spent the remaining time in doing what he could to restore it, and with great hesitation sent it for exhibition. The large cartoon of Caractacus exists in fragments only. Three of these portions are known to be preserved: they were bought some few years later by Sir Walter James (the first Lord Northbourne) from a fine art dealer, and are now at Betteshanger, and with these there is also a drawing of the whole composition measuring 6 feet 3 inches by 4 feet 3 inches. The story of its destruction is briefly this: with the sum of money which had so unexpectedly fallen to his share, the young painter determined to give himself the advantage of going to France and Italy. Just as he was preparing for this Mr. Horsley came to ask for his co-operation with that of the other competitors in a scheme suggested by a fine art agent, who wished to exhibit the eleven prize cartoons in various provincial towns. The agent had made an offer to purchase this collection for a certain sum, amounting, when divided, to something like a third part of an offer already received by the young artist. Finding, however, that if he withdrew his cartoon it might prejudice the value of the collection, he readily consented, and heard no more of the matter until his return from Italy, when he found that the "Caractacus" had been resold to Dickinson the fine art dealer, who had, to his vexation, cut it up into various portions without communicating with him at all on the subject. There exists a smaller water-colour drawing made in part by Charles Couzens, and worked over by himself, and besides this a full-sized picture in oil-colour he had commissioned Couzens to make, upon which he also worked.

Mrs. Henry Ross remembers hearing Mr. Watts say that, whilst this design was in his mind, he happened to be in the Zoological Gardens making a sketch from one of the lions there, and that from the sudden attitude of this animal's head when thrown back for an instant as if at bay, he got exactly what he wanted for the head of Caractacus.

On first leaving England George Watts went to Paris to join a friend of his own age, Edward Armitage, and with him he stayed some six or more weeks in the Quartier Latin. In this way he saw something of the merry life of the young French students of the time, and had very pleasant recollections of it. The name of Edward Armitage was entered as a student at the Academy in the same month and year as that of George Watts, but I think I am right in saying that Mr. Armitage never attended the schools, and studied entirely in Paris under Paul Delaroche.

GEORGE FREDERIC WATTS

The journey to Italy was at that time a tedious and, for those who had to study expense, a disagreeable undertaking. The *Diligence* from Paris to Boulogne took sixteen hours. The *Diligence* itself, though built to carry some fifteen people, seems only to have afforded anything like comfort for three passengers in the body or coupé, these seats being, of course, the most expensive. After this the choice lay between the *Intérieur* with six seats, unbearably hot and stuffy, the dusty *Rotonde*, or the seats outside on the top in the *Banquette*, to be shared with the conductor, but where at least fresh air and the pleasure of seeing the country during the hours of daylight were to be obtained. The journey by *Diligence* from Paris to Marseilles took the wearisome length of four days and three nights, but there was an alternative for travellers who did not object to spending more time on the way. They could leave the *Diligence* at Chalons and go down the Saône and Rhone by river steamboats to Avignon, and so on to Marseilles. It was by this route that George Watts chose to travel, and he found the steamer a great relief after the discomforts of the road. There is a pencilled note, still decipherable, which describes something of this journey; evidently part of a letter written probably to Mr. Armitage, whom he had just left in Paris, a chance scrap of flotsam where all other written record has sunk from sight. It begins: "A Frenchman and a German and myself were the occupants of the *Banquette*. I soon discovered them to be the most favourable specimens possible of the two nations, and we soon became jolly companions. Laughing, talking, and singing much relieved the monotony of the journey, but I defy anything to render the *Banquette* agreeable. I never passed a more wretched night, except perhaps on my passage to Boulogne. Fancy a cold night wind and a horrid disgusting brute of a French conductor, who I had the impression was possessed with murderous monomania, who came and plumped his disgusting corpus in butcher's blouse down by my side, taking the room of six men. We had some snatches of jollity, however, and the second night we behaved so uproariously, singing in chorus the *Marseillaise* and the *Parisienne*, that the proprietors of the *Diligence* took offence at the brilliancy with which we executed some of the passages and complained —the beasts. Thus reduced to silence, we were forced to amuse ourselves by going to sleep, and as I had not slept the night before, Somnus was kind enough to squeeze his poppies on my eyelids."

A tremendous thunderstorm next enlivened that night's journey, and as the *Banquette* had only a rough sort of hood the travellers suffered further discomfort by being thoroughly soaked. With a note in a pocket-book of sundry expenses, and regrets for a mistake which he had made which cost him " a loss of both time and money," there is also a further entry : Monday, September

11, 1843.—"A stranger and an American lent me without being asked £8." On board the steamboat going from Marseilles to Leghorn were English travellers, General Robert and Mrs. Ellice, who also accepted him at sight, and evidently brought a favourable report of him to Lord Holland,[1] then the British Minister at Florence; indeed later on they were the means of his presenting himself at the Legation. They parted at Leghorn, George Watts making his first acquaintance with Italy from an open country cart in which he drove from Leghorn to Pisa. The vintage was in full beauty, as yet ungathered; he recollected at one point driving under a roof of clustering vine, the deep purple bunches hanging from the treillages within the reach of his hand. The weather was divine; those who know Tuscany in September know what he saw — what he felt, — a treasured memory to which he often referred. Also, he did not forget the pleasure of talking in Italian, and understanding his driver's replies.

A few days' delight at Pisa, and then to Florence. It was to have been at the longest a visit of a month or two; but caught away from every thought other than what Florence had herself to reveal to him, the weeks were fast running out when a chance meeting with General Ellice changed the course of events for him during several years. "Why have you not

[1] Henry Edward Fox, son of the third Baron, and his wife Elizabeth, daughter of Richard Vassal. Under this lady's rule Holland House and its circle became famous.

been to the Casa Feroni?" he asked. "Lord Holland has been expecting you, and has caused all sorts of enquiries to be made for you; you must come;" and so urged, to Casa Feroni he went.

The Casa Feroni, as it was then called, is now known as the Palazzo Amerighi, its present number being 6 in the Via dei Serragli. Its date is not more remote than the latter half of the eighteenth century, but it was built by a wealthy son of the traditionally wealthy Feroni family, and is, on a large scale, extending from the Via dei Serragli along the Borgo San Frediano and back to the Piazza del Carmine, enclosing a spacious garden within its quadrangle. It is said to contain a hundred rooms, and one of its chief features is a terrace 20 feet broad running the whole length of the palace and overlooking the garden, the pride of which, now in these days of its departed glory amid broken statues and dried-up fountains, is a grand old pine, behind which comes to view the red dome of the church of San Spirito.

To this house he was invited to luncheon by Lady Holland, and then, as he happened to be on the point of changing his lodgings, the invitation was further extended to a visit of a few days. Lady Holland once recalled this to us, saying, "I remember perfectly well hearing Lord Holland say, 'Why not come here? we have plenty of room, and you must stay till you find quarters that you like.'" This invitation now accepted by George Watts, finally became one to be measured not by days, but by years. It was in this manner that his stay in Italy became a very pleasant one for the young painter, his kind hosts, to whom but a short time before he was a stranger, making him more and more welcome, both to their house in Florence and to their country home at Careggi. The grey mirk of London he exchanged for Italian blue, and the rarely failing sight of " the dear brother sun " of St. Francis, " that greatest of colourists " as G. F. Watts himself called him, while above all Florence gave him the company of her glorious dead.

When thinking of one of the very last times that my husband and Lady Holland met, I seem to hear their voices happily reminding each other of these long past days. She was ill and depressed, but she was roused by those memories, and laughed over stories of this time ; and when he said, pointing to me, " I tell her you let me paint in every room in your house, and you did not let any one else do that," she replied quickly, with a pretty little movement of her head, looking up with youth still in her eyes, " But you were not anybody else."

He never had the slightest inclination to that fine indifference to daubs of colour in wrong places so commonly condoned as part of the artistic nature; a spot of paint where it should not be, vexed him exceedingly. "I feel degraded," he once said, "it is so inartistic" ; and

Lady Holland's quick eye soon perceived this inherent sense of order and care, rooted indeed in a still deeper sense of reverence. She told him that as a girl her mother[1] had taught her the most careful and elementary housewifery—how to dust a room and how a floor should be scrubbed—and she herself saw that nothing in her service was left undone, being up and about in her palazzo at six o'clock to see that what she required of her servants they did.

When such a new element as a painter, with his possibly dangerous paints and mediums, first entered her house, he was pointedly told that he was allowed to use his colours only in the room made over to him as a studio; but not many days passed before these limits were removed. One of the last notes that she penned herself to him begins, "Dear Fra Paolo"—thus reminding him of the first picture he painted at Casa Feroni, a portrait of Lady Holland in a Riviera straw hat, and of the Italian guest, who exclaimed, when it was first shown to him, "Ah, nostre Paolo!" though it is not quite easy to see how the handling of the paint in this picture recalled the work of Paul Veronese.

At no time were the conditions of life happier for George Watts; the climate suited him, he was in much better health, he enjoyed the society at the Legation; most people of note, either living in Florence or passing through, being as a matter of course the guests of the

---

[1] Countess of Coventry, daughter of the fifth Duke of St. Albans.

British Minister. Lady Holland, as he described her, brilliant, full of humour, fond of society, and at that time speaking French and Italian, perhaps even more fluently than English, made a delightful hostess. Lord Holland, large-hearted and genial, was a sympathetic companion, always certain to appreciate what was best in others—a great lover of the beautiful in art and in nature. The young painter made many friends here, and it may be said with truth that he never lost one. Time had taken a heavy toll of years before it was my privilege to meet some of these, but they were his faithful friends still. I remember one lady whose father was at that time attached to the Legation saying, " I was so proud when I was allowed to sit by him at dinner "—and then she added, " and he was *so* handsome."

Lady Holland's *chef* was of course a master of his craft, and encouraged in the display of his talents by his master, who, when a certain *plat* had been considered so successful that the dish was emptied, would call for it and send it down to him with a guinea upon it as the reward of merit. But George Watts, while always ready with a tribute to anything well done, whether it happened to be a housemaid lighting a fire or an artist consummating a great work of art, sat at this well-furnished table, and kept to the ascetic habits of his life: he ate only of the simplest dishes and drank nothing but water, and was amused when Lord Holland told him that for this very reason he would like to have his opinion on some new specimen of wine upon the table. Neither did the pleasant life betray him into idleness; he was at work early and late and accomplished much. He had not been very long at Casa Feroni before he persuaded Lady Holland to sit to him for a portrait, and later he was at work trying his hand at fresco-painting in the courtyard of the Palazzo. His first attempts in this medium have quite disappeared from the walls, but his friend Count Cottrell had two studies for figures painted here (St. John and St. Mary)—and these are now in the possession of his daughter.

In the late autumn of 1844 he saw something of the worst side of the Florentine climate. Torrential rains fell for something like a fortnight, and he recollected that one morning early, as he was preparing to go out, the rain having ceased, he had a message from Lord Holland to say he would like to see him; he found him at a window looking out upon one of the streets, but it was no longer a street, but a fast-running river—a torrent.

Later they stood, not on the Ponte Vecchio, but near it, as the authorities would allow no one to go upon it, and the greatest confusion and anxiety prevailed. There they watched the Arno rise upon the old Ponte Santa Trinità, till a thin streak of light below the arches was alone visible. Had the river risen above that line, the bridge could not have withstood the force of the water. The people, prevented from getting out of their houses by the great iron stanchions covering their windows, were fed for many days by the monks and brothers, who went about in boats distributing food. It was said that no such flood had occurred for upwards of a hundred years.

At a ball given by Lady Holland in the winter of 1844–45, a guest, tired of the weight of a suit of armour he was wearing, went to the room George Watts was using as his studio and took it off. Armour had always fascinated him, and next day he was to be found making a study of it. As the result was a portrait of himself that the Hollands liked, he gave it to them, and it is now at Holland House. At this time he also painted Lord Holland—a portrait unfortunately so greatly injured in 1870, in an outbreak of fire at Holland House, that in spite of much labour on his part he could not restore it to its former worth. A little note from Lady Holland, dated from her house, St. Anne's Hill, January 1871, shows that it was a treasured gift of his to her. "I feel so broken-hearted," she writes, "at the contents of your letter last night that I am almost unable to put pen to paper. For pity's sake, don't take hope from me. Try, oh try, to do something. Call picture-cleaners, picture-restorers, incur any expense—I would starve to regain that portrait. Dear, dear friend, I appeal to your old affections, to the remembrance of days gone by, to every feeling of your kind heart. On that canvas you have still the outline ; you can recall the features of that poor friend who valued you for so many years. What other hand can do what you could do? I beseech you, I implore you, I have lived ever since the disaster in the hope that you would restore me the image of one no longer to be restored to me in life; and will my constant prayers obtain that he be restored to me in another? I have not even that firm faith that many are blessed with." All that could be done he did, and to a certain extent as a likeness it was restored, but as a painting its worth was lost.

His pencil drawings, in number somewhat more than forty, in that same room were fortunately saved; these delicate pencil drawings made by him during the evenings at the Casa Feroni, or at the Villa Careggi, are portraits chiefly of special friends of Lord and Lady Holland; and in later years, in her boudoir at Holland House, she liked to sit surrounded by these friendly faces taking her back to her life in Florence, a time, my husband used sometimes to say, he believed to have been the happiest of her life, English conventions never being quite congenial to her nature. For him, certainly, it was altogether a time he liked to keep green in memory. It was delightful to listen to his account of these happy days: of the pleasant trysts at the Café Doney where he often breakfasted or dined in the company of such men as Hiram Powers, the American sculptor, a hard-headed reasonable man, yet latterly entirely converted to spiritualism; Mr. William Spence, and many others.

He also knew Mr. Seymour Kirkup, who,

under the whitewash on the walls of the Bargello, had made the discovery of the priceless portrait of Dante by Giotto. He often heard Kirkup describe his night in hiding, when he caused himself to be locked up in the Bargello, knowing the portrait was condemned into the hands of a restorer, and he, when refused permission for this, had determined at all costs to make a facsimile of the portrait as he found it, and succeeded in the early morning in making both a tracing in pencil and a water-colour drawing—thus earning the gratitude of the world. The restorer painted in the damaged eye, and made other changes in the features, and in the colour of the poet's dress, which was altered from red, white, and green to a dead brown. Count Cottrell, then Chamberlain to the Grand Duke of Lucca, was one of his chief friends, to whose reverent care is owed the preservation of some hundreds of delightful little studies in pencil and water-colour; these, with several large canvases, were left in the Careggi studio, and were eventually stored by Count Cottrell in the cellars of the Palazzo Torre Arsa, Via Cavour.

Years afterwards Mr. William Spence, writing to Mr. Watts of his colour-men, says, " Bonelli is dead, but there are two or three deformed helps who always grin at the mention of your name"; and in 1853, on his return—after sixteen years' absence—to Florence, the old flower-seller, so long a well-known figure in the streets, on catching sight of him leapt to her feet and ran towards him, till to his dismay he found himself enfolded in her motherly arms and kissed on both cheeks, to the sound of great laughter from his companions, Roddam Spencer-Stanhope and Henry Prinsep.

In one respect during these years (1843–47) he was unfortunate, for Walter Savage Landor was absent in England, and the Brownings arrived at Florence the month he left for home; so that to his great regret he never met Mrs. Browning. Mr. Ruskin passed through Florence and called at the British Legation, but they did not meet until later in London. Nevertheless he had many delightful friends; and of the two in chief who were his hosts he often spoke, wondering if he had been grateful enough, though in all truth he did his utmost to show his indebtedness to them, and to this every picture by him at Holland House bears witness. "I often wonder," he said, "when I think of the kindness of those two to me; as I think of that time I see how wonderfully they made me one with them. It pleases me to think what confidence they had in me, talking to me about their most intimate concerns."

He liked to quote a verse by Shenstone he had learnt from Lord Holland, and wished that he had asked to be allowed to place the words somewhere on a stone at Holland House.

> I prized every hour that went by
> Beyond all I valued before,
> And now they are gone and I sigh,
> And I grieve that I prized them no more.

GEORGE FREDERIC WATTS

One New Year's Day, his thoughts went back to this festa spent at Casa Feroni, and he recalled how those kind friends had wished him good fortune. Lady Holland had sent to Bautte, the famous watchmaker and goldsmith at Geneva, for a watch and chain of delicate workmanship, the only valuables of such a sort he ever possessed; and as she put the chain—then worn long—over his head, she said, " We not only bind you to us, we chain you."

Years later, when he was doing work that took him every day through a crowded part of London, fear of the pickpocket made him take others into use, and he believed he had locked up in safety these, so valued for the giver's sake, as well as for the pleasure he found in Bautte's good workmanship. But they were not beyond the reach of thieving fingers. So vanished his precious watch and chain, and he could never speak of the loss without real pain, nor would he allow any one to replace them.

CHAPTER III

The contemplation of what has been done in art will go no farther to create an artist than the reading of poetry will create a real poet. The artist is born, not made. The latent genius may be aroused no doubt, but, excepting that it is good to know how much can be achieved, the sight of accumulated greatness is more likely to destroy all but the most original power, by making the student an imitator.

G. F. WATTS.

CHAPTER III

As already said, G. F. Watts made his first study of fresco upon the now whitewashed walls of the courtyard at the Casa Feroni.

At the Villa Careggi the fresco painted some two or three years later has been more fortunate. On a blank wall space in a then open *loggia* he found his opportunity. The wall was carefully prepared, and as he had now acquainted himself with the best tradition of pure fresco-painting, he chose for his subject the exciting scene after the death of Lorenzo de' Medici when an attempt to drown his doctor was, or was *said* to have been made. The fresco is lasting well, and has every chance of being well preserved by the present owner of Careggi, Professor Segré, who values it and has made a delightful sitting-room of the former *loggia*. While Lord Holland was minister at the Court of Tuscany from 1839 to 1846, Careggi was his country home. Celebrated from mediæval times, the villa Medicae di Careggi—to give it its correct name—is well known as one of the most historic in the Val d'Arno. The original villa was bought by Cosimo de' Medici, "Pater Patriæ," in 1417, who caused it to be rebuilt by Michelozzo Michelozzi, and by good fortune his work remains almost untouched to this day. During the years that Lord Holland lived there the Roman road still ran by the north side of the house, and its strangely irregular line of wall seems to suggest that Michelozzi chose to keep to the line of the road, and make his great foundations bend to this, much as a man to-day would plant a hedgerow. Whatever reason the great artist may have had for planning this irregularity, certainly the effect of the curving line of frontage, the wall rising grandly to its overhanging gallery under the roof, is surprisingly delightful.

The public road was diverted by a later owner of the villa, Mr. Soames, and trees were so planted that a vigorous young wood now secludes the villa on this side; perhaps rightly, as it has long passed from the glare of a great Court into the quiet shade of private life. Cosimo lived much at Careggi, and died there; so did his son Piero, and again his son Lorenzo the Magnificent, who to its courts and *loggias*, in Plato's name, drew poet and thinker of that great age. The paintings by Benozzo Gozzoli in the chapel of the Riccardi Palace were in all probability almost transcripts of the processions of that date, and present to the mind something of the pageant of colour that may have passed through the gates of this villa, and streamed about beneath its walls in the day of its pomp. Again, but in more sombre colour, Careggi comes upon the page of history when, at the bidding of Lorenzo from his death-bed, Savonarola arrived to make those inflexible conditions upon which alone he would consent to absolve the passing soul. On a summer evening, in the glow beloved by Venetian painters, nature having had time to play delightfully with the modern colour on its walls fretted by the shadow cast by the machicolated gallery, an impression of old gold shining upon a ground of cypress velvet is left on the mind.

And Careggi keeps its fascinations! At least so it seemed in 1910, when its master gave to two travellers kindly welcome, showed them its rooms from basement to roof, and went round the hanging gallery to find points in the landscape made familiar by paintings done by a vanished hand that had worked here with tireless zeal when Lord Holland was the tenant. And at Careggi Lady Holland loved to be, and here she brought the young English painter, who quickly converted a large building in the garden into a summer studio. It was built to shelter lemon trees in winter and was of grand proportions, somewhere about a hundred feet in length; but now the building has gone—pulled down when the villa was in the possession of Mr. Soames. The light was high, with a row of windows so lofty that the painter needed steps to reach his paint-brushes put there to dry in the sun. He remembered how narrowly he had escaped being stung by a viper which had curled itself to sleep upon the handles, and upon which one day when he was about to take his brushes down he laid his hand. In this studio much work was going on, and with a mind attuned to the thoughts of the poets of greater Italy, he designed on one large canvas the story from Boccaccio, now in the gallery of British Art; on another Buondelmonti riding beneath a portico and looking up towards the fair lady whose beauty brought about his murder — the first blow struck in a quarrel between Guelf and Ghibeline, which caused the streets of Florence to stream with blood. Bojardo gave him the Fata Morgana; Ariosto, the Witch pursuing the Knight; Dante, the tragedy of the lovers "whirled ever like driven leaves." The work accomplished in these four years was immense, and the large studio made possible many large canvases. One of these is the picture called "Echo" (now in the Tate Gallery), the under-painting of which is in tempera colour.

The good state of this picture my husband thought remarkable, because for many years for want of wall space it was fastened upon the ceiling of his studio in Kensington, and rather loosely strained upon the stretcher. In course of time it curved outwards like a filled sail; and yet when it was taken down it was solid and whole as when newly painted. "On a tempera ground prepared in Florence," he once said when describing to me the way in which he set to work upon this picture, "I painted a figure in distemper, laying in the skeleton very simply, just the principal bones; these I next covered with the flesh in monochrome (probably in white and terra verte—or it might have been in white and raw umber—I don't quite remember); then, still using distemper, I laid in colour, and finally, using oil colour, I painted just what you see." The ordinary distemper prepared as it is in Italy, is still very superior in quality—so Mr. William de Morgan told him—to the same pigment (whitening with size) as known in England. The studio at Careggi must have held an astonishing number of large canvases. It was always his habit to carry on as many designs at a time as easels or wall space admitted, often in the same hour working alternately on some five or six, or even more, different in subject and in treatment. He found that the change of thought was good, that it kept his mind alert with fresh interest, and that his eye turned with a clearer perception from one to another. Another change for eye and hand he found in modelling, using either clay or wax. The one remaining example of his work in the round belonging to this date is the head of the dead Medusa, which was twice carried out in alabaster, the last chiselling being done by his own hand. The face is that of a noble woman entirely unindividual, one who has suffered in causing suffering; she seems to have welcomed death because it released her from the curse under the spell of which she had turned all warmth of life and youth to stone.

He painted many portraits at Florence, the 2nd Count Cottrell, the lovely Countess Valeska, gifts to the Hollands; that of Mr. William Spence; Madame Ristori; Princess Matilde Buonaparte; Madame Leroux, afterwards Princess de la Tour d'Auvergne. He also paid a visit to Lucca to paint a three-quarter-length portrait of Carlo Lodovico the Grand Duke of Lucca,[1] who gave him his first decoration, the Order of San Lodovico.

A careful study of the work belonging to this time will reveal little mark of change in the style and character of the artist's work as the result of these years spent in Italy. The careful handling, called by a recent writer "hard" when speaking of the portraits at Holland House, was the training he purposely gave himself from the first. Whether the word "hard" should be applied to such portraits as Lady Holland's in the Riviera straw hat, or to that of Panizzi, is an open question. There is certainly an absence of a certain freedom which he allowed himself in his later manner. The representative work done by George Watts at this time will, I think, show no evidence of any great change during his stay in Italy as the result of the more direct influence of the great masters. The characteristics of his portraiture

[1] Now in the possession of the Duke of Parma.

had been, and for many years continued to be, these—an evident avoidance of effort to produce a pictorial effect, an absence of any strong contrast in the shadows, a very evident carefulness of drawing, and the avoidance of any touch of the kind that he would call a smear. There is a portrait in the Compton Gallery of Miss Marietta Lockhart, painted at Florence, to which he specially liked to draw the attention of students, pointing out the absence of shadow, while notwithstanding, all necessary rotundity and projection of the features is preserved.

His long habit of drawing with gold or lead point on metallic paper, a method which admitted of no correction, was, he believed, valuable to him, and this practice he always recommended to students. He discouraged the notion that a student should make copies from the old masters. When he was in Italy he never made a copy of any picture whatever. The water-colour sketches from Titian's "Battle of Cadore," and one from Tintoretto's "Miracle of St. Mark," are the only drawings upon which he bestowed more time than was required to secure small notes in water-colour which he occasionally made from frescoes in the churches. He studied the great masters, but not to copy them. He was convinced that a man who follows another must always lag behind; his aim was to find out the general principle upon which they had worked. In the evidence given by him in 1863 before the Royal Commission on the Academy, he said, "A good general method will never interfere with the expression of genius or trammel originality"; and on being asked if he had himself gained great benefit from the opportunity of studying in Italy, he answered, "Unquestionably it must be so, but I do not think it absolutely necessary that an artist should go to Italy. There are in England quite a sufficient number of works of art to prove to him what may be done, and I think that with these and the Elgin Marbles it is not absolutely necessary that students should travel; but it is obvious that much is to be gained by travelling, the mind must be enlarged by it." That which the young painter gained for his art during his stay at Florence his own words express in writing of Haydon only a few years after he had left Italy. "A visit to sunny climates would have afforded Haydon a valuable lesson. There he would have seen the unrestrained form acquiring that development he could but imagine, and might be excused for exaggerating—the rich colour of the flesh that gives at once the key-note of the picture, the out-of-door life so suggestive of breadth and brilliancy. In Italy to this day, though gorgeous colour no longer contributes its magnificence to the general splendour, one constantly sees forms and combinations that might be adopted without alteration in the grandest composition."

Besides his devotion to his work he found time to enjoy going into society both Italian and

GEORGE FREDERIC WATTS

English, and those who knew him best in his later life of seclusion may be surprised to hear of a little surviving note written by him to his friend Mr. William Spence, saying, " I wish very much to go to the ball to-night, but cannot get hold of a dress. Have you anything of the kind you could lend me?" This might have been the fancy-dress ball at Feroni. He was tasting of the best pleasures that life had to give to a young man, whose looks and manner found favour with most, and music and poetry, in the cool of Italian gardens, were suggestive of romance. It was now that his picture the " First Whisper of Love " was painted, and little scraps of verse belong to this time, written to one who was fair.

Both music and the drama in Italy, during these years, received much support from English residents and travellers. In Florence this was notably the case, much being due to Lord and Lady Normanby. Lord Normanby was the British minister to whose post Lord Holland had succeeded in 1843; they were still resident in Florence, and their interest and encouragement attracted the best musicians and actors, a pleasure that to G. F. Watts was not small. There is a little pencil drawing of the head of Verdi. Madame Ristori was well known to him, and he painted a portrait of her when, as he said, she was a pretty and charming girl. She came to see him again in London in the 'fifties, when he made a drawing of her. Endowed by nature with a fine ear, and answering as he must to everything that was great in any art, he would sometimes speak so enthusiastically of music as to express regret that he had not in early life turned his whole attention to it, rather than to the sister art. Lord Holland liked to tell a story of some one much the senior of Watts, a man of the world, and one who very much believed in himself, who, standing among a group of listeners one day at Casa Feroni, and rather boasting of his contempt for music, turned to those about him — Lord Holland being of their number — and said, "It has not the slightest effect upon me, pleasurable or otherwise — what does that mean, I ask you?" "It means a defective organisation," answered the young painter hotly, obliged, in defence of the divine art, to drop his habit of never putting himself forward. Lord Holland was as much delighted as the boaster was furious.

Though half a lifetime lies between the two utterances, the conviction that brought the quick rebuke to his lips was clearly explained when he wrote the following passage: "'All beauty,' said the devout mystic, 'is the face of God'; therefore to make acquaintance with beauty, in and through every form, is the cultivation of religious feeling. This while it is the noblest aspect of art, is also the most primitive. Nothing can be more important to remember than that in the cultivation of the artistic perceptions we are developing one of the essential endowments of the human creature—one in which that difference between him and the lower creation is most distinctly marked. It seems to me to be the duty of every one to answer to every such call."

George Watts was able also to see something of Italy; he travelled with Lord Holland on several occasions, once driving along the Cornice road to Marseilles. They visited Milan together, and he remembered the Cenacolo as the work which in his opinion placed Leonardo da Vinci as a great painter; for while he demurred as to the popular estimate of Leonardo's pictures, which he thought extravagant, he found in this fresco what he called "the greatest conception of the Christ ever painted." One journey made with Lord Holland was to England, to which in 1845 they together paid a flying visit. During this brief visit to London he saw for the first time Holland House, then in the possession of Lord Holland's capricious mother, Elizabeth, Lady Holland. Though she was living in Stanhope Street at the time, her son had to sneak in at a back entrance, and the visit they paid was made under the rose, as her ladyship objected to her son's going there at all. He brought George Watts an invitation to dine with his mother one evening, but Lord Holland warned him to be prepared for a bad reception, as he explained she made a point of being rude to all his friends. However, that evening she chose to be particularly civil to the young artist. This was the only opportunity he had of being received by her, as she died some months later.

GEORGE FREDERIC WATTS

That evening her sarcasm was so mercilessly directed against her daughter, Lady Lilford, that at last, to the great discomfort of her guests, she reduced her to tears. At another time he drove with Lord Holland to Naples, where he stayed at the Villa Rochella, and on the way stayed both at Perugia and Civita Castellana.

One whole day they spent in Rome; it was a burning day in August, and my husband remembered how Lord Holland, hurrying to give him glimpses of the most famous sights and monuments, still delayed the visit to the Sistine Chapel, the one moment impatiently expected by the painter. His cicerone told him he knew he would be disappointed, for the light was never good enough to see the work, but at last his eagerness prevailed, and they stepped under that matchless roof to find the whole chapel flooded with light. Lord Holland afterwards declared that in all his visits he had really never seen the frescoes till that moment. Perhaps something of this enjoyment may have been due to the companionship of one who certainly had the gift of opening the eyes of those who could share with him the joy of beauty in art or nature. Apart from the walls of this chapel, only by line-engravings could these frescoes be known; and these convey but a small idea of the grandeur of Michael Angelo's style. George Watts, prepared as he was, by all that he had read or heard, for something supreme, was nevertheless unexpectedly overwhelmed. The reproductions

GEORGE FREDERIC WATTS

that photography has made possible — so often pondered over in years to come—once reminded him that Gabriel Rossetti had said that till he saw the photographs he had disbelieved altogether in the greatness of the work. "On the whole, as a complete work by one man, they are the greatest things existing," was my husband's mature verdict; "for we know but half of the work of Pheidias, and we can judge of his greatness only by the fragments that remain, as nothing remains of that which happens to be mentioned in the very meagre written records that have come down to us." He has also said, " Not only does Michael Angelo give a character to his epoch, but he stands for Italy almost as Shakespeare does for England."

With all his reverence for Michael Angelo, he did not place him high as a sculptor, and withheld his praise from the world-famous " David"; indeed, I have heard him declare that in his opinion it was a bad statue—the right foot not good, the waist too small, and the hands not the hands of a youth. He had great admiration, however, for the marble *tondo* in the Diploma Gallery of our Royal Academy; of this *tondo* he wrote to Lord Ronald Sutherland Gower in 1903: "It is a thing of supreme and even pictorial beauty. It is quite lovely being left with a chiselled surface, for it is incomplete according to general apprehension, but in my opinion more perfect, especially the infant Christ, which is as full of sense of colour as any Venetian picture."

To Lord Ronald he also wrote at this time: "My only disagreement with you would be in the estimate of his [Michael Angelo's] comparative excellence in sculpture and painting. He called himself sculptor, but we seldom gauge rightly our own strength and weakness." And later in the same letter he adds: "This seems presumptuous criticism, and you might, considering my aspirations and efforts, say to me 'Do better.' I am not Michael Angelo, but I am a pupil of the greatest sculptor of all, Pheidias (a master the great Florentine knew nothing of), and so far, I feel a right to set up judgment on the technique only." However, for the studies in wax made by this great master he felt an unbounded admiration, and he thought that Michael Angelo was prevented, by the obstinacy of the material, from dashing his thoughts into marble, as he did with the brush upon the walls of the Sistine Chapel.

The Hollands were now often at the Villa Rochella, which had been Lady Holland's home before her marriage, and to her was a very favourite one, long after her widowhood. More than forty years later, when my husband and I looked down from our hotel windows upon the Villa, now surrounded by buildings, it seemed to him that it had been transplanted from the country into the heart of Naples. Men were then busily felling the beautiful ilex and pine of the neighbouring garden, and he turned hastily away, exclaiming, "Don't let us look at it."

Of this delightful first visit Pompeii seemed

to remain most clearly in his mind. His imagination was touched by the signs of life and death in this long-buried city, and by Vesuvius, the great destroyer and preserver of it all, still sending out its columns of smoke as when all was busy in these ancient streets.

He remembered too his scramble up the side of the mountain, when he and only one other of the party (Lord Walpole) went to the top to peer down into the fiery throat of the crater.

He now returned to Careggi and to his work, which went on as earnestly as usual. During the autumn of 1845, when alone, as the Hollands were absent in Naples, I think on account of the illness of Lady Holland's mother, he received the news of the death of his father who had long been in delicate health. A chill, upon which bronchitis followed, was the cause of his death. The previous year his son had returned to England to see his father, when travelling with Lord Holland, who, as has already been said, had invited him to be his companion. Of this sorrow he writes to a friend, many months later: " My father's death has been a sad blow to me, nor have I yet recovered from the effects."

In the following year both spring and summer were entirely spent by the painter at Careggi. Lord Holland having resigned his post at Florence and retired from the diplomatic service, he and Lady Holland spent much time at Naples, and the villa would perhaps have been a little lonely for him in spite of hard work, but that Lady Holland had begged her friend Lady Duff Gordon, with her two daughters, to make as much use of it as they chose. In this way he was again surrounded by that affectionate care which something in his nature required and compelled. When he was unwell Lady Duff Gordon looked after him with motherly care; and he and the daughters, Georgie and Alice Duff Gordon, became great friends over the arts both of painting and music. After the day's work was accomplished, duets and trios often followed; and on a charming old French guitar he played and sang little songs, the words of which he sometimes wrote himself. In the autumn of 1846 they left for Rome, and he was again alone, and at work designing his large picture to be called "Alfred inciting the English to resist the Danes by Sea," where they were considered to be invincible—England's first naval victory. During the summer he had also been in communication with Mr. Ionides about a large picture he proposed to paint for Greece, if Mr. Ionides would supply the cost of the materials.

From Careggi in June 1846 the painter writes to him thus: "If I have not made money, it has been my own fault. With the connection I have made, if I applied myself to portrait-painting I might carry all before me; but it has always been my ambition to tread in the steps of the old masters, and to endeavour, as far as my poor talents would permit, to emulate their greatness. Nor has the sight of their great works diminished my ardour; this cannot be done by painting portraits. Cannot you give me a commission to paint a picture to send to Greece? Some patriotic subject, something that shall carry a moral lesson, such as Aristides relinquishing his right to command to Miltiades, that those who look upon it may recollect that the true hero and patriot thinks not of his own honour or advantage, and is ever ready to sacrifice his personal feelings and his individual advancement for his country's good. Such subjects grandly painted and in a striking manner would not be without effect upon generous minds. Take advantage of my enthusiasm now; I will paint you an acre of canvas for little more than the cost of the material. My cartoon, as you say, was not sold for a large price; I could have got a great deal more for it, but an offer was made to purchase the eleven prize cartoons for a certain sum to be equally divided amongst us, and I did not think it right, by refusing my consent, to prevent those who were less fortunate than myself from making a little money."

There was some correspondence about this suggestion, Mr. Ionides preferring the meeting of Nausicaa with Ulysses, which apparently did not appeal to the mood of the painter. Mr. Ionides having consented to his choosing a subject from Xenophon's *Cyropædia*, he began to paint a picture to be called "Panthea," but this design was afterwards obliterated, and no sketches for it can be identified.

But the question of again entering as a competitor for the prizes offered by the Royal Commission of Fine Arts had now to be considered. All his friends urged him strongly to compete; and he was told that people at home were blaming the Hollands for making him idle. There had been two competitions for which he had not entered. In 1844 the prizes offered had been for arabesques and decorative designs, for friezes, lunettes, panels, and pavements; also for designs to be carried out in wrought iron. In 1845 followed a competition for fresco-painting, six selected artists being chosen, though the competition was open to others. A cartoon, a coloured sketch, and a painting in fresco of some part of the design were required, and three premiums of £200 each were offered. In the next competition (June 1847) the particulars again varied, for the size of the painting was left to the artists, their names need not be concealed, and the medium employed was to be oil-colour.

When he had decided to compete, during this summer and autumn he began to make very careful drawings for his picture of Alfred; and in December he writes to Miss Duff Gordon a very full description of this design. She had asked him to describe it, and he consents to do so as he has "nothing better to write about," and adds that it will be after the manner of the showman. "You ask me to describe my picture of Alfred; the general design you are acquainted with. Alfred stands, as you know, in the centre of the picture, his foot upon the plank, about to spring into the boat. I have endeavoured to give him as much energy, dignity, and expression as possible, without exaggeration. Long-limbed and springy, he is about the size of the Apollo, the other figures are bigger, so you see my composition is colossal. Near to Alfred is a youth who, in his excitement, rends off his cloak in order to follow his King and leader; by the richness of his dress he evidently belongs to the upper class, and I shall endeavour to make that also evident by the elegance of his form, and the grace of his action. Next to him is a youth who is probably a peasant; he grasps a ponderous axe and threatens extermination to the whole Danish race. Contrasted with him you see the muscular back of an older man, who turns towards his wife, who, with a child in her arms, follows distracted at the thought that her child's father is about to rush into danger. He points upward, and encourages her to trust in the righteousness of the cause and the justice of Heaven (religion and patriotism). Behind him two lovers are taking a hurried and tender leave, and beyond them a maiden with dishevelled locks (your sister's hair), whose lover or father has already departed, with clasped hands is imploring the protection of Heaven.

GEORGE FREDERIC WATTS

In the corner a youth is buckling on armour; his old mother, with trembling hands and tearful eyes, hangs about his neck a cross; the father, feeble, and no longer able to fight his country's battles, gives his sword with one hand, while with the other he bares his chest, points to his wounds, and exhorts his son not to disgrace his father's name and sword; while with glowing cheek and beating heart the youth responds to his father's exhortations with all the ardour characteristic of his age. This I think my most interesting group. I have made the parents old and infirm and the young man but a lad, in order to show that he is the last and youngest, the Benjamin of the family; his brothers, we will suppose, have already fallen fighting against the Dane, defending their country. You see I endeavour to preserve a rich base accompaniment of religious and patriotic feeling. A boy, carried away by the general enthusiasm, clenches his little fists, draws his breath, and rushes along with the excited warriors, which helps to indicate the inspiring effect of Alfred's harangue. In the foreground two men lift from the ground a bundle which has been provided by the prudence of the king. On the other side of the picture some men, impatient of delay, rush through the water and climb the vessel-side, while others are engaged in getting it under way. Now I think you have an idea of what my picture is intended to be."

GEORGE FREDERIC WATTS

He made numberless pencil drawings for this picture; some forty of these are preserved (mostly owing to Count Cottrell's care), none of them measuring more than twelve inches at their longest dimension; sometimes the figure of Alfred is repeated five times on the same bit of paper, and the whole group, in most careful outline, is drawn over and over again whilst he considered various changes.

He was much absorbed in this picture, which he described in a letter as "dedicated to patriotism and posterity." Work must have been incessant, as on December 21 he writes that the painting is not yet begun, and only the studies are made; yet by April 15 he was on his way home with it almost completed, and during this short time he went to Rome for a fortnight. He had been driven away from Florence by the intense cold of that March, but returned hurriedly to Careggi when he found that there was little time to spare. On April 15 he started from Leghorn, going home by sea, and taking with him five canvases varying in size from twenty feet downwards. He left Careggi meaning to return in a few months, though a foreboding that he should never see it again is shown in a letter of good-bye to Miss Duff Gordon: "I reply to your kind letter and say farewell to Italy at the same time. The boat is steaming away in the harbour, my place is taken, and in a short time my back will be turned upon my beloved Italy. I grieve to leave it, particularly at this moment, when it is beginning to put on all its charms. Careggi was looking beautiful. Dear Careggi, I may never see it again ! though it is my intention to return, if possible, immediately ; I am too well aware of the accidents to which the future is subject to count upon anything." And so it was ; when he went back to Italy, sixteen years later, Careggi was in the possession of strangers and he could not bear to revisit it.

CHAPTER IV

THE artist must bring to his work the ardour of the young lover or the missionary. No matter what his artistic organisation, if he is satisfied with a few hours' hard work—no matter how hard—and can throw thought of it aside and say he has done enough for the day and will throw aside "shop"; not for him will be a place on the highest level for all time.

G. F. WATTS.

CHAPTER IV

ONCE more in London, George Watts did not decide upon taking a studio, as his intention was merely to pay a short visit and to return to Florence immediately after he had been able to arrange matters for his two stepsisters, and when the big picture had been completed and placed at Westminster Hall for the competition in June.

In the meantime Mr. R. S. Holford, the well-known connoisseur, kindly offered him the use of a large empty room at Dorchester House. He had made the acquaintance of Mr. Holford at Careggi during the last months spent there. A letter of introduction from the Duff Gordons having taken a fortnight to reach Careggi from Rome, he did not receive it until the day after Mr. Holford and Mr. Reginald Cholmondeley had been to visit him, when, as he writes, he was much puzzled, first by the Italian servant's version of their names, and then by being expected to welcome them. However, stiffness was soon at an end: "We plunged into art; the dear and only love was hanging upon the wall; I prosed away about Pheidias, they listened with politeness; I mentioned Giorgione, they went off in their turn; my own pictures were forgotten, I don't recollect whether I showed them—if I did, I am sure they don't recollect seeing them. Finding them such enthusiasts, I promised to go next day into town, and carry them to the house of an old gentleman whose acquaintance I have lately made, and who has some of the finest pictures in the world. Accordingly this morning I breakfasted with them and Lord Ossulton, and afterwards introduced them to the pictures, which are wonders. Mr. Holford will never survive if he does not carry off the Giorgiones." This bond of enthusiasm soon made them, he says, "old acquaintances," and the result of this introduction was that he was for some time provided with a temporary studio. Having now no home in London, he found rooms for himself at 48 Cambridge Street; these he kept until 1849, when he became tenant of the studios at 30 Charles Street, Berkeley Square. His stepsisters had, on the death of their father, removed to the country, and, as he writes before leaving Italy, he wished to see that they were comfortably settled; but the father's loss had greatly loosened the tie to his old home. In spite of a considerable difference of age, the father and son were the two who completely understood each other, and certainly they were one in a search after something that seemed to each never to be attained. The father, bent on making music through some new channel—an adaptation of wind upon strings—so I seem to understand it—but never able to perfect his invention, in the bitterness of his disappointment, finally broke up and utterly destroyed the whole fabric upon which so much had been lavished. The son also, from his earliest days, was bent—so it were possible—upon making the world richer by the music of another art. With the sisters, for whom he had now arranged the matter of an income for their lives, it was different. "There was a difference of fibre," as he expressed it, existing always, but probably much accentuated by the years of absence in Italy, and later by unhappy friction, greatly due, as I have been told, though not by him, to the temper of one sister; so that the breach ultimately widened until they had no part in his life.

In June of that year, 1847, the exhibition of competing works was opened. The names of the three winners to whom were awarded first premiums of £500 stood as follows:—

To F. R. Pickersgill for his picture, "The Burial of Harold"; to George Frederic Watts for his work, "Alfred inciting the Britons to resist the Landing of the Danes by encountering them at Sea"; and to Edward Armitage for the picture, "The Battle of Meeanee."[1]

[1] Upwards of forty years later Sir F. Burton told me that he remembered well this competition for the decoration of the Houses of Parliament, and how when he came away he said, "We have two men who will do well—Watts and Stevens."

On the close of the exhibition Sir Charles Eastlake recommended the purchase of four of the pictures for the nation — Pickersgill's "Harold"; Watts's "Alfred"; "Richard Cœur de Lion," by J. Cross; and "The Battle of St. Vincent," by W. A. Knell — to be placed in committee rooms of the House of Parliament. In his letter to the Treasury Sir Charles Eastlake says: "With respect to the prices of the four pictures selected, the Commissioners have directed me to acquaint you that Mr. Watts had intimated his readiness to present his work to some national building or public institution. The Commissioners were unwilling that the picture should be obtained on such terms; their wish to purchase it, with the sanction of the Treasury, arose from their high appreciation of its merits, and was altogether uninfluenced by the views of the artist. Mr. Watts, when invited to fix a price, named £200 only, explaining his reasons for doing so in a letter of which a copy is annexed. I am directed to request the sanction of their Lordships to the proposed application for £1300 for the pictures above named." The letter enclosed by Sir Charles to Her Majesty's Secretary of the Treasury is as follows :—

"Sir—In accordance with your request that I should distinctly put a price upon my picture, I have again considered the subject. I will not occupy your time by repeating the reasons I before submitted to you for declining to name a price, but will content myself with saying that the distinction and amount of the prize awarded to me is more than sufficient recompense and payment for my labours; that if I may not have the honour of placing my work at the disposal of the Royal Commission, I wish to name a sum which, by not drawing too largely upon the funds devoted by the Government to the encouragement of art, may leave it in the power of the Royal Commission to extend to other artists the honour and advantage of having their works purchased by the nation. In naming as a price £200 I trust my intentions may not be misunderstood,—that it will be seen it was my desire to assist the object of the Royal Commission, and by no means to establish a precedent prejudicial to the interests of the profession.—I am, Sir, your faithful and obedient Servant, G. F. WATTS.

In November the picture was moved into a convenient light in one of the committee rooms, where Mr. Watts was allowed to work further upon the figure of Alfred; Sir Charles Eastlake had made some suggestions which he thought well to carry out. It now hangs upon the walls of a committee room in the House of Lords. The choice of this subject, England's first naval victory, with its dedication "to patriotism and posterity," indicates the trend of his desire throughout life to be numbered amongst those who had dedicated themselves to the service of their country. He expressed this hope fifty-two years later, saying to me, "If in the future any one writes of me the little there is to say, I hope that they will say, not that I had painted many pictures, but that my strongest feeling was for the honour of the nation."

It was at Dorchester House that he painted "Life's Illusions" and "Time and Oblivion"—this being the first realisation on canvas of the dominant idea of his life to deal in art with the great problems of human existence. In 1897, when turning away from the door of the New Gallery where his work was collected, he said, "Only two pictures there seem to me to come near my mark—'Time and Oblivion' and 'Life's Illusions.' Of 'Time and Oblivion' I think Pheidias would have said, 'Go on, you may do something.'" Of this picture he also said, "I never did anything better, but discouraged by those who alone regarded art seriously, I did not go on working in the way that I believed in; I lost many years of my life for this reason."

It was whilst he was working at Dorchester House that he and Mr. Ruskin became acquainted. Mr. Ruskin greatly cared for this picture, asked that it might be lent to him, and had it hanging on the wall of his house in Park Street for some time; but, gradually becoming more and more in love with the faithful rendering of fact, this prepossession seemed for a time to obscure his vision, and his mind closed against the view held by Mr. Watts, that in imaginative and poetic painting certain material facts must be sacrificed to convey the impression, exact imitation being then out of place.

Seeing that the picture had ceased to please him, Mr. Watts asked that it might be returned. Years afterwards it was bought by Lord Somers, and is now at Eastnor Castle. It was exhibited at the Academy in 1864, and described in the catalogue as "A design for sculpture, to be executed in various materials."

Of the difference of opinion upon these points between Mr. Ruskin and himself he writes: "I have been thinking a great deal about your remarks and the tendency of your criticisms, and I cannot help inflicting some tiresome observations upon you, not, I beg you to understand, with any reference to my own things: my own views are too visionary, and the qualities I aim at are too abstract, to be attained, or perhaps to produce any effect if attained. My instincts cause me to strive after things that are hardly within the province of art, things that are rather felt than seen. If I worked to please myself only, instead of making a weak and insufficient compromise, I should make outline compositions filled up upon a monochromatic principle, and in my most elaborate efforts aim at nothing beyond the highest and noblest beauty of form, truth of movement, and general colour. I confess that, failing so greatly, my work never gives me the slightest pleasure. I cannot bring myself to labour upon a thing that disgusts me, and my instinct rebels against imitation. I will do a bit some day just to show you I am capable of it. Perhaps it is not necessary to say all this about myself, but I want you to feel and believe that my remarks are made not as an artist, but as an amateur. Like you, I am most interested in the progress of art, and believe it can only be great by being true; but I am inclined to give truth a wider range, and I cannot help fearing you may become near-sighted. That I feel with you with regard to earnestness and truth in painting must be evident from my agreeing with you in admiration of certain productions; but I do not agree with you in your estimation of truth, or rather your view of truth. It appears to me that you confound it too much with detail, and overlook properties; and that in your appreciation of an endeavour to imitate exactly, you prefer the introduction of what is extraneous, to the leaving out of anything that may be in existence. Beauty is truth, but it is not always reality. In perceiving and appreciating with wonderful acuteness quality and truth of accident, you run some risk of overlooking larger truth of fundamental properties. In fact you are rather inclined to consider truth as a bundle of parts, than truth as a great whole.

"I venture to say this to you, because your opinion has great weight, and your judgment is listened to with great respect; and I want you to consider well, and walk round the truth, viewing it from the distance as well as examining it with a magnifying glass, lest your eye and taste, becoming microscopic, fail at length to take in the length and breadth."

The answer to this letter has not been preserved; possibly it may have been as a verbal discussion, perhaps prolonged over many meetings. The two friends were often in combat, though on each side there was great appreciation—certainly on Mr. Watts's side unbounded reverence,—but upon principles of form they differed to the end, and had many a passage-at-arms. In the volume collecting Mr. Ruskin's "Notes on Pictures" the editor (Mr. E. T. Cook) says :—

"In a letter of the year 1849 Ruskin wrote to a friend : 'Do you know Watts? The man who is not employed on Houses of Parliament—to my mind the only real painter of history or thought we have in England. A great fellow, or I am much mistaken—great as one of these same Savoy knots of rock ; and we suffer the clouds to lie upon him, with thunder and famine at once in the thick of them. If you have time when you come to town, and have not seen it, look at "Time and Oblivion" in his studio.'"

As I read to my husband one day, I remember that he stopped me to say of Mr. Ruskin, "How earnestly he pleads for all that would develop the best in humanity. Never let us be a week without reading something of his. In another generation he will be placed as the greatest thinker of the age. As a teacher, his theories are opposed to political economists, but are truer, because they are based on a belief in the best side of human nature. It seems to me in taking this for his starting-point he is perfectly right."

Though not in its place chronologically, the following letter shows that through many years the two friends were at variance upon this matter of realistic truth and essential truth, a point of great importance in judging of my husband's work. In a note of mine made after a visit to his studio in the 'seventies, I find the following: "Signor told me to-day of his meeting Mr. Ruskin outside Burlington House during a winter exhibition of the works of old masters, and how, in a discussion they had, Mr. Ruskin had said that these great men were all wrong, because they did not paint exactly what they saw; and, denying that there were any truths more essentially true than surface facts, said almost fiercely, 'Paint that as it is,' pointing to a scavenger's heap of mud lying at the foot of a grimy lamp-post; 'that is truth.' They walked for some way discussing, and, before they parted, Signor rather hoped that his friend had come to be somewhat convinced by his arguments; but a letter followed next day, Mr. Ruskin probably suspecting his thought.

GEORGE FREDERIC WATTS

"Bull Hotel, Piccadilly,
but usually
"Brantwood, Coniston, Lancashire.

[Postmark, 13*th February*, 1873.]

"My dear Watts—I am sometimes a little hypocritical in conversation. I took laughingly your charge of losing sight of all the points of things while I pursue one. But—seriously —you ought to know me better. I challenge you (so far I am proud of what I have done though not of what I *am*) to find any writer on art ancient and modern—whose range of sight is so microscopic and yet so wide as mine, and when you fancy I am losing sight of things, they are continually most in my mind. But I purposely veil every other part of my subject, that my reader may understand one at a time. As for breadth of sight, do you suppose there is any other man, even among your most thoughtful and liberal friends, who can not only admit but intensely enjoy the good in De Hooghe and in Luini—in Reynolds and Angelico—in William Hunt, and Tintoret?

"But not one of you—even of my best friends—have the least idea of the work I have done, privately, in getting my knowledge of my business; nor have you any notion of the power it gives me now to have steadily refused to be warped from the sight of the pure facts by my likings. . . ."

(His lash here descended on others of his

particular friends, and he then turns again upon G. F. Watts.)

"You fancy you see more than I do in Nature—you still see less, for I, long ago, learned how impossible it was to draw what I saw—you still struggle to do so; that is to say, to draw what you like in what you see without caring about what others like—or what God likes.

"In saying all this, I retract nothing of what I said of my discontent with myself, nor do I equal myself for an instant with Jones and you in personal power of thought and deed. I merely speak as a poor apothecary's boy who had earnestly watched the actual effect of substances on each other might speak to (when he got old, and did know precisely what gold and lead were) two learned and thoughtful physicians, who had been all their lives seeking the philosopher's stone.—Ever affectionately yours, J. RUSKIN."

It was at Dorchester House that the picture called "Michael the Archangel contending with Satan for the Body of Moses" was begun; it was never carried out to completion, but is a suggestion of the two figures standing in a great light. Though fresco-like in quality, it has also such atmospheric qualities as might make an expert, some hundreds of years hence, place it chronologically as work belonging to the latest years. In this respect it differs

GEORGE FREDERIC WATTS

much from "Time and Oblivion" and other work of this period. Mr. Ruskin cared for this picture sufficiently to buy it, about 1849–1850. Through the kindness of Mrs. Severn it has lately returned to the studio at Limnerslease. He also painted his Miltonic Satan with the face averted from the light of the Creator with whom he talked. For title, these words were used: "And the Lord said unto Satan, Whence comest thou? Then Satan answered the Lord and said, From going to and fro in the earth and from walking up and down in it." The Satan the painter conceived is a mighty power ruling over the evils which were unconnected with sin.

At this time also, in the days of her youth and beauty, Lady Waterford[1] came to sit to him. The portrait was to be a present from him to the Duff Gordons—but a labour of love paid back a hundred-fold by thus making him acquainted with this gifted lady.

"For certain he has seen all perfectness who among other ladies hath seen her. She walked with humbleness for her array; seeming a creature sent from Heaven to stay," are the words upon her grave chosen to express the greatness of her nature by those who best knew her. That characteristic of "humbleness," expressing itself by a little touch, a very slight touch, of hesitation in manner and speech,

---

[1] Louisa, Marchioness of Waterford, whose memoirs, with that of her sister Lady Canning, are to be found in Mr. Augustus Hare's book, *Two Noble Lives*.

appealed much to him in one so richly endowed both by nature and fortune.

Of her genius for art he has said that he believed she was *born* an artist greater than any England has produced, the circumstances of her life alone preventing her from working on to the full achievement. What work she did accomplish was, as far as it went, of the very highest order. Her brush full of colour, so unerringly blotting in all that she knew was essential to her subjects: these were always poetical, imaginative, and dignified, beautiful in colour and in arrangement of line. No faltering about truths of proportion and movement, or in the disposition of masses: nothing to jar as being out of keeping with the conception of her subject. He hoped that some day examples of her work would be preserved in one of our national galleries. The intercourse now entered upon was carried on intermittently throughout her life; and, until illness prevented her moving from Ford Castle, she often came to find him at work in his London studio. They also met at Blickling, but he never visited her at Ford; and memoranda of trains by which he never travelled, written out by her own hand, still lie in some of his old blotting-books. This portrait of Lady Waterford was one of the gifts he made to what he sometimes called "The Casa Gordon," and they were not a few; for, from the happy Careggi days when the acquaintance with Lady Duff

Gordon and her daughters was first made, delicate little pencil portraits and paintings in water-colour were frequently bestowed upon these friends. Many letters passed, usually in a most cheerful tone; but in one he becomes more serious, and defines the points that in his opinion a student and lover of art should regard as most important. In the autumn of 1847, having heard from Miss Duff Gordon that she wished to study art more thoroughly than she had as yet, he bids her "set about it in the right way; if not, the harder you work the more laborious will be your idleness; all the energy and power of endurance will not enable a man to reach his journey's end, if he be not on his right road. It must first be your object to separate the essence from the material, to discover in what consist those qualities which affect the mind, and what their properties. I say discover, for no man can teach that great point: Pheidias himself could but direct the attention, and lay down simple rules. No poet was ever formed in a school. . . .

"The mere mechanical difficulties are always to be overcome by the means of judicious and continual practice. The elements of the beautiful and the elevated are the real difficulties. Master them, and fill the mind with the contemplation of what is great; the hand may tremble, but it must obey the impulse. But it is not the knowledge of proportion, it is not the knowledge of the rules of poetry that will make the Pheidias or the Homer. . . . I cannot think real greatness compatible with the existence of mean passions, hence the impossibility of attaining perfection. But I have allowed my subject to run away with me, I have been prosing away at a great rate, when I merely intended to say that the technical difficulties of pursuing a course of study would not prove formidable."

Lord and Lady Holland were now living at Holland House, and deeply interested in restorations and improvements there. The hospitable door was as open to Mr. Watts as it had been in Italy. He was much there, Lady Holland reserving a room for him, and he in return throwing himself into their interests, and doing all in his power to give them pleasure. He restored the ceiling in the Gilt-room, and painted upon both ceilings of what was then known as the Inner Hall: *amorini* on the first, and on the second, figures and a balcony representing mediæval Florence. Guizot sat to him there at this time, and he also persuaded Lady Holland to let him paint a full-length portrait of her, or, as she called it, a "full shortness." In this picture he introduced, what is unique in his work, a mirror in the background to reflect the plaits of her auburn hair. His two portraits of the librarian of the British Museum, Anthony Panizzi, belong to this date; they were painted at the Museum. One of these is at Holland House; the other

GEORGE FREDERIC WATTS

he reserved for himself, and it is now in the National Portrait Collection. He was also working upon his two big pictures, "Life's Illusions" and "Time and Oblivion." Other designs were in his mind, such as "Death and Resurrection," "Satan, Sin, and Death," and "Charity giving the Water of Life to thirsty souls," "Satan calling up his Legions," and the "Temptation of Eve," where she and Adam lie asleep, while above them on spread wings Satan hovers and whispers in the ear of the woman. There is also the drawing named by him "The people which sat in darkness saw a great light," a design for a fresco never carried out. Taking shape in his mind at this time was the scheme which may be described as the ambition of one half of his life and the regret of the other half. He called it later "The House of Life," and at a very early stage tentatively outlined this conception in words a fragment of which in faded ink remains. It runs thus :—

"The ceiling to be covered with the uniform blue of space, on which should be painted the Sun, the Earth, and the Moon, as it is by their several revolutions and dependence upon each other that we have a distinct notion of, and are able to measure and estimate, the magnitude of Time. The progress of Time, and its consequent effect, I would illustrate for the purpose of conveying a moral lesson — the design of Time and Oblivion would be exactly in its place. To complete the design, the Earth

GEORGE FREDERIC WATTS

should be attended by two figures symbolic of the antagonistic forces, Attraction and Repulsion. I would then give, perhaps upon one half of the ceiling, which might be divided with a gold band on which the zodiac might be painted, a nearer view of earth, and by a number of gigantic figures stretched out at full length represent a range of mountains typifying the rocky structure or skeleton. These I would make very grand and impressive, in order to emphasise the insignificance of man. The most important (to us) of the constellations should shine out of the deep ultramarine firmament. Silence and Mighty Repose should be stamped upon the character and disposition of the giants ; and revolving centuries and cycles should glide, personified by female figures of great beauty, beneath the crags upon which the mighty forms should lie, to indicate (as compared with the effect upon man and his works) the non-effect of time upon them."

Reduced to the dimensions of a picture, some ten feet in length, now hanging in the National Gallery of British Art, there is a characteristic representation of this idea. Torn from its true setting, and named by him "Chaos,"[1] there is enough to show the painter's largeness of style and imaginative power, and perhaps to make some minds regret that the spirit of Pope Julius II. was not alive in England to give him the

[1] After he had presented this picture to the National Gallery of British Art, he regretted not having chosen the word "Cosmos" for the title.

walls of a Sistine Chapel on which to consummate his greatest conception. The manuscript continues:—

"Then I would begin with man himself, trace him through his moral and political life; first the hunter stage, gaining, through the medium of his glimmering yet superior intelligence, advantages over the stronger yet inferior animals, almost his equals. Next the pastoral state, his intelligence further developed to the consequent improvement of his condition: serviceable animals domesticated, reclaimed by his thoughtful care, the stronger and finer subdued by the force of his will, aided by all-conquering intelligence. This is the Golden Age, the age of poetry. Of experience comes tradition, of tradition is born poetry, here performing its natural and legitimate function—instructing. This portion of the work might be rendered most beautifully, since in this period of the history of society it is possible the human animal enjoyed the greatest possible amount of happiness, equally removed from the penalties of ambition, and from the degradation of a precarious and merely animal existence. There would be a great chance of exquisite subjects to illustrate this epoch, and here might be introduced the episode of Job.

"Next should be man,—the tyrant—the insidious oppressor—the slave, a dweller in cities—the Egyptians raise the pyramids—their mythology—the habits of the people."

GEORGE FREDERIC WATTS

The manuscript seems roughly to indicate that his first scheme was to end in a pageant of the progress of civilisation through Palestine, Assyria, Persia, India, Greece, Rome, each with their mythology and their representative men: the dawning of the Christian era; the fall of Jerusalem; the history of the Middle Ages in Europe; the rise of the Saracen power; the preaching of Peter the Hermit. As the idea developed in his mind the scheme became more abstract, and less realistic and historic; it is certain that as the mythology of the races was traced by him, its place would have been prominent, and possibly the whole scheme would have developed into the history of the progress of the spiritual side of man's mind; and he would simply have niched the men whom he considered most representative of all forward movement.

The fragment quoted belongs to a very early stage of the conception of this scheme. In later years he writes of the work he had been able to accomplish as "only to be called a series of reflections mainly upon ethics. With certain material advantages, which would have caused me by their nature to weld my thoughts into a regular form, I think my efforts might have been given place as an epic." As he described it, it seemed like some magnificent dream; a magnificent dream, yet not at all impossible of realisation had enthusiasm been stirred in the right way, and directed in a practical manner.

GEORGE FREDERIC WATTS

Perhaps it was asking too much of his contemporaries that they should see any use for such a Temple of ideas : at the moment the public was satisfied by, and understood best, the expressions of decorative art, to be found housed in a giant glass building. The æsthetic and spiritual emotion of the time, led variously by Keble, Newman, F. D. Maurice, and Charles Kingsley, found different satisfactions. The great preacher Thomas Carlyle had not the vaguest sense of the proportionate value of great art in the history of civilisation. To Mr. Ruskin, as well as to the Pre-Raphaelite Brotherhood—his true brothers in devoted service to art—he failed to make his aims intelligible. With the greatest reverence each for the other's achievements, there remained a difference : neither the mediæval nor the theological nor the decorative point of view was his.

To the question of what gifts the painter could have brought as his contribution to "The House of Life," an answer must now be found in what he always considered to be but scattered pages torn out here and there from some book which had cost a lifetime to compile : the first page—to carry on this figure of speech—to be the picture called " Chaos," and the last, " Destiny," begun in the latest working hours of his life, and destined to be left unfinished.

In the winter of 1848 he was on the point of paying a visit to Greece, travelling with Mr.

Ionides and returning to Italy; but, because of the disturbed state of Europe, this journey had to be given up, and during the following year he established himself in a large studio at 30 Charles Street, Berkeley Square, moving his pictures from Dorchester House—I believe on account of alterations and rebuilding in progress there. And here, surrounded by the large canvases, "The Muffin Pictures" as he called them (alluding to the skit by Thackeray on the painter in *Our Street*), he went to work still hopeful. Below this studio was another he found himself able to lend to a miniature painter and copyist, called Charles Cozens. They had known each other as boys, and Cozens, being greatly influenced in his work by that of his friend, obtained commissions and occasionally made copies of G. F. Watts's portraits, as these were frequently required by the Ionides family.

By this time he had many acquaintances and friends, and young men whose names were afterwards distinguished were often in that studio. When Sir Robert Morier came to see my husband in 1891, they talked much of the friends who used to gather there and at his rooms in Bond Street. Chance accidents preventing, they had not met for about forty years; but the friendship was fresh and alive as ever, and Sir Robert declared that his face was quite unchanged—" singularly so," he said to me.

Sir Robert Morier believed that this group of friends met first at his rooms in Bond Street.

G.F. Watts

from a photograph of a drawing, now lost, made about 1848

GEORGE FREDERIC WATTS

Subsequently it would seem that the meetings were at Colonel Stirling's,[1] and it seems probable that when war was declared and Colonel Stirling left for the Crimea, the friends to whom the studio in Charles Street was well known during Mr. Watts's tenancy, applied for these rooms and there established the club that became known as the Cosmopolitan. Amongst the earliest members of this club Sir Algernon West mentions Edward FitzGerald, Francis Palgrave, Monckton Milnes, Henry Reeve, Danby Seymour (the owner of " Life's Illusions "), Lord Goderich, Julian Fane, Philip Hardwicke, and Henry Phillips the painter (honorary secretary of the club).

The members with whom my husband was best acquainted, and whom he recollected meeting at Mr. Morier's rooms were: John Ruskin, Henry Layard, Vernon Harcourt, Tom Taylor, Chichester Fortescue, James Spedding, Thomas Hughes (?), Henry Phillips, and Lord Arthur Russell. For many years his picture " Echo," the story from Boccaccio, and an " Early Study," a sort of Arcadian picture, hung upon the walls of the club-room. Sir Robert told us that at one time, when the finances of the club were not flourishing and a considerable outlay was necessary, to avoid this expense they moved to other rooms; but they so missed the associations, and the pictures, that members began to

[1] See Sir Algernon West's article on "The Cosmopolitan Club" in the volume entitled *One City and many Men*, and also his volume of *Recollections*.

give up going there, and signs were evident that it was falling all to pieces; so to pull it together again, they spent a far larger sum of money, and returned to the original house, 30 Charles Street. In 1902, when the club removed, the members generously presented the large picture which they had bought to the Tate Gallery, and the Arcadian picture was returned to my husband and is now in the collection of his works in the Compton Gallery. The painting called "Echo" he had claimed many years before.

Amongst the congenial friendships begun at this time was one with Mr. Aubrey de Vere, a life-long friendship, for until his visits to London had to be given up, Mr. de Vere came yearly to spend some hours with his friend. The wife of the poet Sir Henry Taylor (Miss Alice Spring Rice), a cousin of Mr. de Vere's, had brought these two poetic minds together. Mr. de Vere, in his hours of uncertainty before he decided to join the Church of Rome, had often paced the studio in Charles Street (1849-50) pondering this question. Perhaps with intuition thus quickened he knew that his friend was also passing through a time of crisis. However that may have been, Mr. de Vere, writing from Coniston in October 1850 to arrange with him to go to Curragh Chase at the invitation of his brother Sir Vere de Vere, says: "You would find much to interest you deeply in Ireland, besides its scenery, including not a little of which you must have had a second-sight vision before you painted your 'Irish Eviction'" (afterwards called "The Irish Famine").

A few days later, with further plans, Mr. de Vere writes (doubtless referring to something in his friend's reply to the former letter) : "To fortune you may well be cold, especially if she is cold to you. Fortune, like other flirts, can only be made amenable by being paid in her own coin. 'The lion on your own stone gates Is not more cold to you than I,' so sings Tennyson to the foolish beauty. Fortune is commonly only kind to those who, like poor Byron, have a great wish to be spoilt. Those who have every greatness in them are not attentive to her, and the energies which are to end in conquering the minds of men are trained at first by conquering her petty caprice. She will do you little harm, though she will somewhat delay your harvest, and it is better that she should be unkind to you than to those who are more easily disturbed or depressed. The office of genius is to do good and receive good—not from men ; so you must begin by doing good to Ireland, who will thank you or misunderstand you, just as accident may determine."

To Mr. Watts, Ireland was of great interest, and he remembered being vexed by the ordinary tone of the Members of Parliament who sometimes appeared early in the evening at Holland House, explaining that only "those tiresome Irishmen" were speaking, and consequently they had been able to come away. To Ireland he went, staying at Curragh Chase, where, as they were going upstairs one evening, he drew a little figure—a recollection from Flaxman—on the wall, in charcoal, meaning to rub it out next day; but instead it was carefully preserved, and was still in existence when, forty years later, Mr. de Vere told me of it. From Curragh Chase he went on to Dromoland, where Mrs. O'Brien, Mr. de Vere's sister, invited him. When there he made a drawing of Sir Lucius O'Brien. No doubt his friend thought that it would be a good move for the young painter to get away from London, good for his health, and good for his mind. Mr. de Vere's letter shows that Mr. Watts was already missing the sunshine of Italy—his health was not as good as it had been when there; his visions of "The House of Life" were fading before his eyes; he was liable to be depressed and to gibe at Fortune for being unkind. This visit was a delightful one, he had many a scamper across country; and a letter written to a niece of Mr. de Vere's—Mary O'Brien—shows him in his merriest mood, one that to the last the "delightful people," as he sometimes expressed it himself when speaking of children, never failed to bring him.

"30 Charles Street,
"Berkeley Square, London.
[1851]

"My dear little Mary—I was delighted to receive your nice little letter and pretty present, for which I fill this letter with thanks, and if you don't find them in it they must have dropped out at the post-office. The purse is beautiful, but it has one defect, which is, when all the money is taken out of it, it is empty ; now if you can send me a purse that will always be full, you can't think how I should value it ! In the meantime I am very grateful for this one, which I shall always keep for the sake of Mary O'Brien and my first visit to Ireland, where I should now like to be playing at Brush with little Irish boys and girls. Your great card house was prodigious ! what a pity you could not send it to our great glass-house exhibition as a specimen of Irish industry ! I hope you have missed me on rainy days and riding expeditions ; I have very often wished I could take a good jump and come down right in front of Dromoland. Pray remember me to your Grandmama and your Aunt, and your Mamma and Papa. I am glad you have beaten him at chess ; do you remember how shamefully he locked us all up one day ?—but we gave him plenty of trouble though. How you will enjoy your visit to Curragh ! I should like to go and see you all there, and as I shall be all the summer at Liverpool[1] perhaps the temptation will be too strong to resist—will you undertake to get up a subscription of welcome for me ?

"I have only seen your Aunt Grace once and that was on Saturday, for I have scarcely been

[1] The work at Liverpool was not undertaken ; as, before anything definite had been decided, the commission for a fresco in the House of Lords had been arranged.

in London at all. When you go to Curragh Chase do not forget to tell your Aunt that I cannot get any of those songs I was so fond of, in London, nor over in Brussels. I owe your Uncle Aubrey some letters—do you think the purse will enable me to pay that debt?

"I wish I knew something extraordinary or interesting to tell you, but as I don't I must finish my letter with all this paper to spare. Mind you remember me to all; you may kiss the smallest of the children for me if you like, and the largest too while you are about it, but that will be if they like; one thing you must certainly do, and that is always believe me to be—Yours most sincerely and affectionately,

"G. F. WATTS."

Mr. de Vere in 1896 retold for my benefit a story of heroism which should never be forgotten. Of this I made the following note: " After luncheon Mr. de Vere came in; his visits give one a pleasure apart from all others. To-day as he sat by us, his short silver curls shining in the light, his clear bell-like voice and pleasant enunciation, I thought how well his name Aubrey de Vere described him. I love to see him by Signor, they are absolutely harmonious. Asked to repeat the story of courage, one that Signor could never hear too often, he told us of his niece Mary O'Brien, who as a child of twelve had shattered a finger when playing with gunpowder. She wrapped it up and said nothing about it, but her mother insisted on seeing it, and at once sent for a surgeon, who said the finger must be cut off. 'Well,' she answered, 'if that is so, please do it quickly, for papa will be home in half an hour.' She then begged her mother to leave the room, and on her refusing to do so, she said, 'Very well, then, don't look at my hand, look into my eyes and then you won't mind.' No wonder that a boy of fourteen hearing the story became her boy-lover on the spot and her husband in after years."

Mr. de Vere remembered that when he first visited the studio in Charles Street, he had said, as he was leaving one day, "You must feel great joy in the fact that you have such close affinity with the great Italian masters, for certainly their mantle has descended upon you"; to which the answer was, "Ah, well, if I have received a mantle at all from them, it was only after it had been quite worn out!"

It was about this time that he first proposed to himself to paint the distinguished men of his time, and so to form a collection to leave as a legacy to the country. For this end he sometimes thought of approaching the Duke of Wellington and asking him to allow him to paint his portrait, but a certain hesitation as to whether it would be acceptable or not prevented him from writing, and the request was never made. One of the very first of this series was painted at Holland House about this date—

the head of Lord John Russell, now in the National Portrait Gallery; and also the drawing of Sir Henry Layard, and that of Mr. James Spedding made in the studio in Charles Street, to which some of his most interesting and beautiful sitters came. Lady Holland had said, "I never know my friends until you have painted them"; and though Mr. Ruskin twitted him with turning his sitters into angels when they were not, it can hardly be doubted that so shrewd an observer well understood that his friend had a power of compelling his sitters to the highest mood of which their natures were capable. Some one has said, " Mr. Watts paints people alone, and with their best thoughts." To those who knew him best, the meaning of the word *alone* went further; it meant that they had met somewhere, somehow, where the barriers of individual self fell away, and they talked to him as if to their own souls. "They look upon me as nobody," he used to say, laughing, as he turned to explain matters to some one who might be by, when a beautiful fair-haired angel or two happened to flit in, and enfolded the painter in their arms as naturally as they would have enfolded some darling child—one of the commonest, but one of the highest tributes paid to his high nature, and sign of theirs. "I think people do care for the desire, there is nothing more in me to care for," he told me one day, always feeling a wonder why he was held dear by so many friends.

GEORGE FREDERIC WATTS

No outline of his personality can be at all adequate without the attempt being made—if also in mere outline—to describe an exceedingly elusive, but at the same time distinguishing characteristic, which the word charm does not entirely cover; it was this, that the Seer in him, or, if it must be called by the more modern name, the transcendental Self, was always visible. Intensely human as he was, understanding all in the lives of those about him—the most trifling difficulties and the most profound—entering gaily into the merriest mood or the manliest sport, the presence of this transcendental Self was always apparent. Everything about him seemed an expression of this, and if touched by some thought of specially wide reach from a friend or from a book, the contact with his imaginative Self sent a sort of transfigured look into his face, as if a flame had been lighted.

Knowing nothing of psychical phenomena, it is not for me to suggest any connection between this visionary quality and three unaccountable incidents which happened to him in these years. Of any psychic faculty he was not in the least conscious, he never encouraged anything of the sort in himself by going to séances or making acquaintance with mediums. Strange things happened to him, he knew, but how they occurred, or what they meant, he did not attempt to explain. The first of these adventures was at Careggi, and bears on the face of it such possibility of a practical joke, played by an undiscoverable though no ghostly being, that it need not be recounted here. The second was different. It happened when he was walking home late one evening to the house of Mr. Ionides, who was then living at Tulse Hill. Coming to a long stretch of pavement, walled in for the villa gardens on each side of the road, a very plainly dressed woman in a plaid shawl went along the pavement before him, and very naturally his eyes were fixed upon the folds of her dress, taking note of the varieties of shadow and the play of light as she passed under the light of several street lamps. As the hour was late he was walking quickly, and therefore overtook her, and he just turned in passing to glance at her—*but she was not*. He stopped, astounded to find himself alone, looked forward and backward, examined the wall to see if there was any way through it, but there was none, nothing but a stretch of blank wall, lighted by the lamp that was close to her and to him when she vanished. He told his friends of this strange experience, but no story of murder or other tragic occurrence connected with that place was ever heard of.

An even more strange and more beautiful thing out of the mysterious came to him during the first months of his tenancy of the Charles Street studio. At one end was a staircase with a landing leading to his bedroom door. One night, hearing a sound for which he could not

GEORGE FREDERIC WATTS

account, he got up from bed, and without a light went out upon the landing, standing quietly there to listen. He then became aware that the sound he heard was the sound of wings beating against the vaulted ceiling of the studio, and that as they circled round and round, a voice cried softly; "*anima mia, anima mia,*" now farther, now nearer, and then all ceased, and there was perfect stillness. "It seemed to me then," he once said, "that it was a soul seeking its own essence." It was no dream; the sound of the fluttering wings and the voice that he heard were as real to him as the floor that he stood on, or the wall against which the wings beat.

CHAPTER V

Love of art almost implies sympathy, since its productions are as much to give pleasure to others as to ourselves, unless it has been debased to a mere trade.

G. F. WATTS.

CHAPTER V

INTO the three or four years of the painter's tenancy of the Charles Street studio a good many events were crowded, all of which fall with importance into the story of his life. He was working hard and refusing all temptations to go into society, though many doors were open to him at this time; but one day, being at Holland House, he fell into conversation with a man much about in London—a Mr. Fleming—who happened to mention the beauty of a certain young lady, Miss Virginia Pattle, now living in Chesterfield Street, as he explained, with her sister and brother-in-law, Mr. and Mrs. Thoby Prinsep. To them he declared Mr. Watts must be introduced; but for answer he pleaded want of time, and his intention not to make any new acquaintances, and so the matter dropped.

Not long after this, it came about that in the neighbourhood of Charles Street he happened to pass two ladies walking with a little boy. All three were in the matter of good looks so much out of the common—the younger lady especially so, her long grey cloak falling in beautiful lines against her tall figure—that Mr. Fleming's description of the beautiful Miss Virginia Pattle came into his mind, and he felt certain that he had now seen her. He went home and wrote to Mr. Fleming that he believed this had happened, and that now he was as eager to be introduced to the Prinseps as Mr. Fleming had been to bring this about. The letter was shown to Mrs. Prinsep, and he was accordingly invited to their house, 9 Chesterfield Street. Being near Charles Street, they soon saw much of each other, and the acquaintance thus made rapidly passed into a friendship.

Artistic to their finger-tips, with an appreciation—almost to be called a *culte*—for beauty, the sisters were quickly at home in the studio, and in love with the work and its aims. "I was never dazzled by any other painter's brush," I remember Lady Somers once telling me, adding, with a smile, "all other brushes were like boot-brushes to me."

The dress of the sisters was not quite of the fashion of that time, but designed by themselves upon simple lines; it depended upon rich colour and ample folds for its beauty, and was very individual and expressive. Many were the admirers who sat at Miss Virginia's feet, both men and women. "Her smile lighted a room," Mrs. Erskine Wemyss once said to me, having known her in her youthful beauty. The first portrait for which she stood

The Countess Somers
1849

to Mr. Watts is in delicate silver point, the long grey cloak falling about her with all the grace that he had seen on that first morning; the next almost a profile outline also in silver point, showing the deep lids drooping over the beautiful eyes. But these studies are many, one so minute that her sister, Mrs. Cameron, always carried it inside her watch-case. Through all the adulation she remained unspoilt and unaffected—" great," as her painter used to say, " in the absence of self-consciousness."

Mr. Prinsep was now a Member of Council at the India Office, having returned to England after some thirty-five years' work in India—one of several brothers who had laboured there with distinction. Large and philosophic in mind, grand in his stature, his learning, his memory, his everything, even to his sneeze! (once received with an *encore* from the gallery of a theatre), childlike in his gentleness and in the sweetness of his nature, it was no wonder that Mr. Watts was quickly attracted to him. In after years he deeply regretted that of the many literary men who knew Mr. Prinsep well, none had left any description of a man so remarkable for his endowments. He remembered the Poet Laureate, as he rose to go, having ended a long hour's talk one day with his friends then living at the Briary at Freshwater, exclaiming in that sonorous voice of his, and with the deliberation that gave such weight to his words, " Well, Thoby, you are a wonderful man." "He was," my husband said once, "an encyclopedia of valuable information on every sort of subject. It was just like turning the pages of a delightful book, and, like it, open if you wanted it and shut when you did not. Like a child in the perfect unconsciousness of his wonderful knowledge and absence of display—as simple as a child, and with its charm."

It will be granted, however, that there is a whole biography in the portrait head of him painted in the early 'seventies, and now amongst the collected works in the Watts Gallery at Compton, Surrey;[1] and further that it reaches the painter's own standard of true portraiture, that of finding the man behind the surface. The surface is there rendered as it was in life, the blood circulates, the bones lie beneath, but the man is there also: the brain at work, the eye alive with thought; and yet through all these appears the charm of his childlikeness.

Mr. Thoby Prinsep will live in this portrait, as also in the drawing made in charcoal when he was a much younger man about 1850–52. These were the friends into the centre of whose life George Watts was gradually being drawn, and, amidst the unseen flow of events carrying him to this haven, none perhaps had more force than that he was again slipping back into a bad state of health. His old enemy of headache and

---

[1] The portrait was generously given to this gallery by Mrs. Andrew Hichens.

nausea had returned, and so violent were these attacks that, while they lasted, he would lie quite motionless for hours, with almost the look and the pallor of death upon his face.[1]

This, of course, appealed to the large mother-heart of Mrs. Prinsep, with her genius for all sorts of confections in the way of delicate foods, and endowed as she was with untiring energy, especially where nursing was required.

A serious and prolonged illness of this nature, which was then described as a nervous fever, befell him during the early months of 1850, with a threatening of paralysis. Throughout this illness Mrs. Prinsep took care that he was well nursed, and during his convalescence both sisters were constantly with him. It was decided that he was to have the advice of Dr. Gully at Malvern, the Prinseps being already there. On his way to join them he spent some days at Eastnor Castle, and the beautiful Virginia and her sister drove over to fetch him from the place which was afterwards her own home. It is said that Lord Somers—then Lord Eastnor—first saw her portrait in Mr. Watts's studio and fell in love with it. However that may be, he certainly captured the original, and they were married in October of this year, 1850.

Many were the reminiscences I used to hear of her forty years later. "Oh, how in love with her we all were!" Lord Aberdare exclaimed

[1] This description was given to me on separate occasions, but in almost the same words, both by General Arthur Prinsep and by Mrs. Ross (Miss Janet Duff Gordon).

once, turning away from a charcoal drawing, perhaps the portrait that above all others renders her beauty to the utmost—the face in full view, life size, and with eyes deep as the night sky.

Sir Charles Newton, amongst others, used to break out into reminiscences, and point to this picture and that, saying, "It was painted when my friend Watts and I, in company with several others, were deeply grieved by the thought that Lady Somers had married; we thought she ought not to marry any *one*." It was at this time, perhaps under an impulse to make an effort to conquer his own depression, by going beyond self into the sufferings of others, that Mr. Watts painted three or four pictures of such sorrowful sort as "Found Drowned," the wreck of a young girl's life, with the dark arch of the bridge she had crossed from the seen to the unseen, the cold dark river, and the deep-blue heaven with its one star watching all. "The Irish Famine" (which at this date Mr. de Vere calls "The Irish Eviction," so possibly its title was still uncertain) was painted over and obliterated another design, called "Panthea," a more splendid subject from Xenophon's *Cyropædia*; also "Under a Dry Arch," a dying woman with all the anguish of a long life scored upon her face; and perhaps "The Seamstress," recalling Thomas Hood's "Song of the Shirt," though this picture was completed later at Little Holland House.

There was much to sadden him; the want of

response, except amongst his own personal friends, to all the enthusiasm with which he had returned to England, full of faith in a revival of great art, was making itself felt with chilling effect year by year. In a moment of depression he writes: "I do not expect at most to have the opportunity of doing more than prepare the way for better men—and not that always; more often I sit among the ruins of my aspirations, watching the tide of time. Will not that explain somewhat the picture you call the 'Seashore'?" No wonder that in such a mood he once signed "Finis" in the corner of one of his pictures. But the challenge to despair was given by Mr. Ruskin, who, on reading the word, took up the charcoal and added beneath, "*et initium*." If the end, then a beginning; and so it proved to be.

During the autumn, finding that for various reasons Mr. and Mrs. Prinsep were anxious to live more in the neighbourhood of London, and not in it, Mr. Watts took them to see a house now to be let, known as a sort of dower-house of Holland House, in which Lord Holland's aunt, Miss Fox, had lived for many years with her cousin Miss Vernon; and the result was that on December 25 a lease of twenty-one years was entered upon, and in January they established themselves there.

Little Holland House, with its rambling passages and many stairs and quaint rooms, showing clearly that formerly two houses had been made one, had its garden and fine trees and its paddock, and beyond again the farm, which later Mr. Prinsep also rented, lay only two miles from Hyde Park Corner, with much untouched country still around it.

The place had its history: Miss Fox had entertained most of her brother's friends there—Macaulay, Mackintosh, Coleridge, and others. Jeremy Bentham was her friend, and report says that he wished to marry her. The glimpses given to us are of a most lovable lady, and her uncle Charles James Fox had a great affection for her. To Little Holland House they carried the dying Lord Camelford from the field behind it, after the fatal duel that he had himself provoked with Mr. Best, and there four days later he died. Its windows looked out upon the field upon which Cromwell and Ireton had walked discussing affairs so secret that they chose this remote spot, in order to prevent Cromwell's words, when speaking loudly to Ireton, who was deaf, from reaching other ears. The twenty-one years' lease now held by Mr. Prinsep, and in the end extended by four more, was destined to be the last of the old house, but if this latest chapter of its life could have been written, it would have in no way diminished in interest.

How Mr. Watts came to live there was once picturesquely described to me by Mrs. Prinsep: "He came to stay three days, he stayed thirty years," she said, with a little descriptive action of her hand; and it seems a pity to destroy such dramatic summing up by mere fact. But Mr. Watts's recollection was different, and he felt certain that the arrangement was made from the first. Perhaps neither memory was quite at fault, the arrangement most likely being proposed at first, but not carried out, and some months later initiated somewhat accidentally.

In girlhood Mrs. Prinsep and her sisters had lived in France with their grandmother, Madame de L'Étang, whom, by the way, Mr. Watts remembered seeing, when upwards of eighty, down on her knees in a passage in the house in Chesterfield Street, keenly interested in playing a game of chuck-halfpenny with her great-grandsons. Madame de L'Étang had solved the problem of education for her granddaughters by having them taught all sorts of housewifely arts, rather to the neglect of lesson-books and accomplishments. Listening to Mrs. Prinsep's description of her early life, and her regrets that she had had what she called "no education," riveted all the while by her power of vivid description and her originality of expression, one could but acknowledge the perfect success of the omission. It was a remarkable group of sisters, each so individual in her own way. The eldest, Mrs. Jackson, had now become known to Mr. Watts. The intimate friend of many literary men and women, she also seemed to me in her old age to be the most beautiful of the sisters; for, as my husband explained to me, the structure of her face was so fine that the beauty of line only increased with age. A drawing of her was in the Royal Academy Exhibition of the year 1850, as well as one of her daughter Adeline. With these he also exhibited his picture, the "Good Samaritan," dedicated to Thomas Wright, the Manchester philanthropist, an account of whose labours Mr. Watts read in turning over the pages of *Chambers's Magazine* while having luncheon at some restaurant. The work for discharged prisoners, later to be so greatly developed by Lord Shaftesbury, was begun by this man. While earning a daily wage in a cotton manufactory, with a large family to support, his attention was drawn to the case of a poor man who earnestly desired to re-establish himself honestly after having been in gaol, and who was being driven out by the strong prejudice of his fellow-workmen. In the end the managers gave him his discharge, and though this was rescinded on Wright's intercession, it was too late, and the man had already gone they knew not where. The "Good Samaritan" is described thus in the catalogue : "Painted as an expression of the artist's admiration and respect for the noble philanthropy of Thomas Wright of Manchester." It was given with this dedication to the Town Hall of that city, and a few months later Wright himself appeared, bringing Mr. Watts a thank-offering of six pocket-handkerchiefs. He also gave him the great pleasure of hearing that the presentation of that picture, having called attention to his work, had been already of great service to him. Seeing that the head of Wright was remarkable in its refined and spiritual beauty, he asked if it was possible for him to give a sitting of an hour or so ; with the result that a drawing in black and red chalk—now in its place in the National Portrait Gallery—was made in the Charles Street studio, and there Wright is niched amongst men who have made their mark.

"The Saxon Sentinels," painted at Dorchester House, was at this time exchanged for a little piano ; this picture being afterwards sold to Mr. Burton of York by a dealer in the Strand, it disappeared for some time. It is believed that Mr. Burton stored the picture and forgot the painter's name ; but under his will it passed into the possession of the Corporation Gallery of York. It was there rediscovered by Mr. Marion Spielmann, who recognised it from the description he remembered hearing from Mr. Watts. At the same time he began, but never completed, a companion picture, which he called "Bayard and Aristides," choosing these as representative men.

In 1852 Mazzini was brought to his studio by one who cared much for the picture of "Time and Oblivion." To this friend Mazzini had maintained that it was not possible for a picture to have any moral influence, and denied that it could have intellectual suggestions, after the manner of a poem. However, he came, and, after looking at the picture, confessed that he had been wrong, and that the painter was working in a new way.

Still anxious for wall space upon which he could fresco some subject worthy of commemoration, he asked Lord Elcho to be mediator. Acquaintance with him had first been made in Florence in 1843 when, on their marriage tour, Lady Anne and Mr. Frank Charteris—as he then was—came to the Casa Feroni. The great hall at Euston Station had been built, and Lord Elcho approached the Chairman of the London and North-Western Railway on the subject of allowing his friend the painter to decorate it on condition that the railway company should pay for scaffolding and pigments. The Chairman stated privately that even such expense was not justified by the state of the company's finances: the architect was much alarmed, and declared that he and the directors would probably be stoned if such a scheme were sanctioned by them. It has somehow come about that, in mentioning Mr. Watts's offer to fresco Euston Station, recent writers have made the mistake of saying that it was there he intended to paint the history of Cosmos—the House of Life. Reading a statement of this sort once to him, he told me very positively that "it was entirely disconnected with Euston, for this remained a vague idea never taking any particular form through want of encouragement."

Meantime the Fine Arts Commissioners offered a small space, in all only thirty feet long and divided into six compartments, to the same number of painters, in which subjects from Chaucer, Spenser, Shakespeare, Milton, Dryden, and Pope were to be painted, "with a view to the future decoration of the Palace of Westminster." Unfortunately there were many objections to this scheme. Where space was so limited, to accomplish a good result by means of six different minds, at work on different themes from six different poets, a kind of patchwork must have been the inevitable result. The light reflected by means of mirrors from the windows above the pictures was exceedingly bad; moreover the corridor was in frequent use, which was most disturbing. Mr. Watts was so little satisfied with what he was able to accomplish that he wrote to Sir Charles Eastlake, offering either to repaint his picture under more favourable conditions, or, as he says, "to paint some other space instead, if Her Majesty's Commissioners will give me permission; and this I should consider a very great favour indeed, and I would not venture to make such a proposal but that, regarding the whole work as a national one, I feel that every individual member has a right to offer his best services, and I can never consent to leave in the House of Parliament, or indeed anywhere else, anything that is not as good as I can make it." Unfortunately these panels were destined to rapid decay. I do not know to what cause it has been attributed.

I think I understood that these were not

pure fresco paintings; anyhow, in 1858 Mr. Watts saw the first symptoms of decay, the colour peeling off the plaster, not only in his own fresco but in Mr. Cope's also. At the present time, as the mischief was beyond repair, the remnants of the six paintings are entirely covered up from view. Some very delicate pencil drawings, done at this time by G. F. Watts, and two sketches in oil-colour for this design, called by him "St. George overcoming the Dragon," are preserved, so is the cartoon; though greatly damaged. These are sufficient to show the artist's conception of Spenser's "Triumph of the Red Cross Knight," when

> All the people as in solemn feast
> To him assembled with one full consort,
> Rejoicing at the fall of the great beast
> From whose eternal bondage now they were releast.

Of this composition he writes: "I fear it may be thought too crowded; but I would venture to defend this as being characteristic of the poem, the intention and style of which, it appears to me, the artist should endeavour to illustrate, rather than any particular incident."

About 1852 a remarkable Greek was in London—Theophilus Kaïrus—and some of his compatriots, Mr. Watts's friends, were anxious that he should be painted. A young Greek once told me a story that had grown up about this portrait. Kaïrus, he said, had refused to sit, and it had therefore been quietly arranged that he and the painter should meet at dinner, and

GEORGE FREDERIC WATTS

be seated opposite each other. Mr. Watts had come, and had eaten nothing, but had given his whole mind to the study of his subject, and so without further sittings had accomplished his fine portrait. My husband, when he was told this, said that it might be partly true, though he did not remember how far it was so; but he added that Kaïrus certainly sat to him several times. He was of the type of an old Greek philosopher, wonderfully good and noble. Because of his religious views he was prosecuted, sent to prison, and thereby ruined, as he depended on his school for a livelihood. The original portrait was lost; it was lent to a copyist, who finally pawned it, and it utterly disappeared. Mrs. Coronio[1] had a replica of this picture.

Still urgent for wall space, in June 1852, having seen the blank spaces on the walls of the great Hall at Lincoln's Inn, Mr. Watts wrote to make a definite offer to the Benchers as follows:—

"Believing that no man of liberal education denies or undervalues the importance of art, at once the test and record of civilisation, it is still a disgrace to us that, while in literature, in science, and in arms we are second to none in the highest and noblest branches, our painting and sculpture can lay claim to no very great excellence. This I am certain is not to be attributed to want of talent. Long reflection and extensive comparison of the different schools

[1] Aglaia Ionides.

and epochs of art have convinced me of the importance of mural decoration as a means of developing those qualities which would place British artists by the side of British poets, and form a great national school. It is with these views and in the earnest desire to apply what little talent and acquirement I may possess to useful purposes, and feeling that no man of intellect can prefer dumbness of language and blank spaces to the eloquent literature of art, that I venture to make to the Benchers and students of Lincoln's Inn the following proposition, namely, if they will subscribe to defray the expense of the material, I will give designs and labour, and undertake to paint in fresco any part or the whole of the Hall." Owing mainly to the representations of the architect of the Hall, Mr. Philip Hardwicke, the hearty consent of the Benchers was obtained, and the fresco was begun in the following year, and went on intermittently whenever the courts were not sitting. Whilst waiting for this opportunity the painter was keeping his hand in—so to speak—by decorating the walls of Little Holland House, in company with Mr. Roddam Spencer Stanhope, who in the summer of 1850 had been introduced to him by Dr. Henry Acland,[1] who wrote: "He is the Commoner of Christchurch of whom Newton spoke to you as an aspirant amateur draftsman. You will be pleased with his simplicity and *bonhomie*."

[1] Later Sir Henry Acland.

GEORGE FREDERIC WATTS

A glimpse of their companionship at this time has been given in letters from Mr. Stanhope to his people at home.[1]

"I am undergoing what Watts terms the discipline of drawing. . . . I am at work now upon a towel scattered in a picturesque way upon the floor, and which Watts has enjoined me to draw with as hard a pencil as I can get, and shade with the finest lines possible, in order to study and imitate everything I see upon it, even to the blacks.

"He says the first object is to acquire power in representing any object whatsoever upon paper in black and white, and this is the surest and quickest way of arriving at this facility. After that has been obtained, the rest is comparatively easy—anatomy, study of form, etc., being most necessary, and painting may follow close upon that. He recommends me to draw lots of outlines as well, carefully and decidedly, and without rubbing out; but to avoid drawing even from the antiques indiscriminately, and he says it is a sure way of spoiling one's taste for form. He seems to approve of few besides the Elgin Marbles as lessons to study from." As I copy these words of advice given in 1851, I feel how entirely they represent the views he held to the end of his life—the advice given in the 'seventies to me, and again so often repeated when students came to him during

[1] Quoted by Mrs. Stirling in her article entitled "Roddam Spencer Stanhope," *Nineteenth Century and After*, August number, 1909.

the last years of his life. One gathers from this letter that Mr. Stanhope had accepted his views as to the value of daylight; for he writes that he breakfasts at a quarter past seven, and gets to the studio in Charles Street about eight o'clock.

"About one o'clock I find myself at Little Holland House, where I do a little in the way of luncheon, and when that is cleared away Watts and I set to work, which we carry on till it is nearly dark.

"Watts, now I know him, is a glorious companion, and the Prinseps are very jolly people."

Although in the letter of introduction from Sir Henry Acland the desire is that the relations between them should be as master and pupil, I think it may be said with absolute certainty that Mr. Watts never did undertake to give more than a certain direction either to Mr. Stanhope's studies or to those of others. "I never had a pupil in the true sense of the word," he often said; and I remember Lord Carlisle turning round suddenly when talking to him, and laughing heartily, he walked down the studio to where Mrs. Percy Wyndham and I were, and explained, "Signor has just told me he never felt advanced enough himself to take a pupil." The position is—so it seems to me—made clear by Mr. Stanhope himself, who writes—and this in 1853 after working beside Mr. Watts some eighteen months: "You see what I have done in the way of study has been all original, and without the aid of masters. I think Watts is right; he is very fearful of influencing me in any way, and never makes a comment upon anything I show him, but only urges me on, and gives me good advice about keeping in the right way."

The relationship between them, in Mr. Watts's eyes, would be that of fellow-students; as he had the advantage of years and experience, he believed that he might have principles to give to the younger man, but this was all. Lady Elizabeth Stanhope, anxious about his influence upon her son, "moral as well as artistic," is reassured, partly because her son thinks most highly of his character; partly because he tells her of the giant-stride in Little Holland House garden—she calls it a merry-go-round —where the three Prinsep boys, their tutor, with Roddy and Watts, go round and round till they are quite exhausted; and she adds, "*very innocent.*" Then, after Mr. Watts had given up his studio in Charles Street in September 1852, she invited him to stay with them at her son's request, mentioning that after his kindness to "Roddy" this cannot be refused, and she is still further reassured. "Watts is as quiet as a mouse," she writes, "working from morning to night, and is not an expensive guest, as he drinks nothing but water." I rather think that his friend Henry Phillips may have taken over the studio, or else the Cosmopolitan

GEORGE FREDERIC WATTS

Club allowed him to make use of it at times, as he seems to have made appointments with his sitters in Charles Street as late as September 1853. It was probably about this time that he built his first studio at Little Holland House. A gap between two walls was filled up by him, and this was his working studio, though in the heat of summer he found it too sunny, and for this reason he built another later, on the north-west side. This studio shows to the left on the drawing of the old house from the north-east.

In May 1852 Dr. Acland had asked Mr. Watts to consider the idea of filling a spandril in his house at Oxford. He suggested that an outline of a composition by Flaxman, a particular design for which Mr. Acland had a great admiration, might be suitable for the space. The design was one taken from Flaxman's illustrations to Hesiod, engraved by Blake. To this request Mr. Watts replied in a letter a copy of which exists; it is dated from Little Holland House, May 8, 1852. In it he says: " I should find it very difficult to reply suitably to your most kind letter, and I will not make the attempt. I know that you do not intend to flatter, and therefore take that which would really give me great pain as an over-estimation of my abilities to be only a proof of sympathy with my views and aspirations, and as such most gratifying and encouraging. I am most sincere in my wish to do good, for many years grieving to see art without a mission or an aim, and ardently desiring to awaken some remembrance of its legitimate purpose and real use. Professionally I have neither interest nor ambition besides the furtherance of what I feel to be a worthy object in any way that I can imagine, or in any way that may be suggested. The most that I can expect is to be instrumental in preparing the way for better men, and I am right glad to see upon the walls of the Royal Academy this year ample evidence that these will not be wanting. Meanwhile I will paint and send you a picture from Flaxman to fill up the space you offer. I was sure you would duly admire the great productions of that fine genius."

This spandril is now in the Ashmolean Museum. In 1902, on receiving a letter from Oxford inquiring about the spandril, my husband told me that Sir Henry Acland had greatly admired this particular design, and that in consequence he drew it out on a large scale and laid it in flat colour for him.

"Flaxman had no sense of colour, that was his great fault; his outlines were superb," my husband once said to me. "It was the lack of this sense that made him blind to the beauty of the Elgin Marbles. In the best sculpture you feel the palpitations of colour, the elements of a picture; you unconsciously see it painted! His work was beautiful on a small scale, but on larger work he was all abroad. Actual dimension has an impressiveness all its own.

"Accustomed to draw in outline on a small scale, Flaxman overlooked the fact that the simple mass that had such a good effect in his outline would be, when put into stone, but a lump of stone, not representing flexible conditions or colour."

In June 1852 Sir Charles Newton, writing from Mitylene, where he had lately been appointed Consul, tries to entice him there.

"Why are you not here? If you could but see my cave by the seashore, where I lie all through a summer's day, and read Shelley. All nature shut out by the over-hanging rock except one blue bit of the Mediterranean, which comes in little summer waves, splashing at my feet. All through my siesta I hear the monotonous murmur, which has continued to lull weary mortals to sleep since the time when in these islands was the cradle of Greek civilisation. I am getting very fond of the place; it would suit you exactly. I feel that the landscape before my eyes is the landscape which Homer saw, and has described in his similes, and which Pheidias turned into beautiful impersonations in sculpture; here there is no sensation of collision and conflict between the elements and man. His physical frame and the nature around him, though different in kind, seem so completely in harmony that we are for ever reminded that we are parts of one great system. I gaze at the landscape till my very soul seems absorbed and blended into it, till I forget the material constraints of the body. No wonder that the ancients made death beautiful; who would hold any other faith in such a climate? Have you finished your fresco? [St. George, in the House of Lords]. When will you come out to me?"

This must have been a great temptation to the man
> Who in that monstrous London dwelt,
> And half-remembered Arcady,

and he writes in reply: "Indeed I could find it in my heart to desire no better fate than to dream away my life in such an isle as Mitylene, but I repress the half-formed longing. I wish you here very much daily, nay, hourly; we have views and sympathies in common, and I see with great interest and satisfaction the time approaching when the principles I have so long worked for, and which you with more dexterity and power were beginning to dash into shape, may be carried into effect and brought to bear upon a useful purpose."

But in the autumn of the following year he allowed himself a month's holiday, and in company with Roddam Spencer Stanhope and Henry, the eldest son of Mr. and Mrs. Prinsep, he went back to his beloved Italy. After a day or two in Paris they left for Marseilles—no dreadful *diligence* experience this time; but the railway was not open beyond Chalons, so he again went down the Saône and Loire to Avignon, where trains were available, and so on to Marseilles. They saw something of Genoa on their way to Leghorn, stayed at Pisa and Florence, and went thence by *vetturino* to Bologna, Padua, and Venice. These two last-named places he had not seen during his former stay in Italy. I find a fragment of a letter from him beginning :—

"My dear Ruskin—I have been to Venice : you are right"—here the rest of the sheet is torn off, but on another side the letter continues : "I can better understand now why I fail ; Titian, Giorgione, and all the most glowing and gorgeous translations of the Venetian School have rendered Nature as I feel her—as I too would render her—but my imagination is not vivid, nor my memory powerful. In Venice especially the exquisite colour of the time-tinted stone against the splendid sky gave me ideas of combinations such as I have scarcely ever seen even in those great masters I have named. The fine bearded heads, grandly coloured chests and limbs every moment being presented to view, made me long for colours and brushes. Under the influence of the glowing sun every object is presented in a manner so in harmony with my own feelings that the whole language of Nature seems to me perfectly intelligible." And here the fragment ends.

In another note on this journey his enthusiasms awake and are crying out :—

"Then ! the glories of that Golden House,

the Cathedral of St. Mark's, more, to my thinking (no critic as I am), like a house not made with hands than anything I ever saw; with its uneven pavement and walls, its strange antique mosaics, and the more modern ones of equally high import and more beauty: not pictures, but representations of heads, arms, legs, or draperies—the large utterance of a majestic language—how impressive, how intelligible is the whole! When the rays of the setting sun passing through the windows of one side of the dome illumine the opposite side, the effect is wonderful—wonderful in the variety of colour and ornament. Below, niches that seem to be scooped out of solid gold are thrown into depths of shadow by massive projections. Upon the broken surface of gold, bright spots start out like gems, as some tessera on the surface presents a different plane to the light. As the eye travels upward to that part of the dome in full light, by contrast it looks like the glory of heaven itself. Such wealth of material, boundless profusion, and reckless scattering of variety is a rendering of nature's joy. I had not imagined it possible to attain such completeness of design with apparent absence of it; largeness of whole, with its marvellous impression of unity, profusion without confusion, finish without smallness, contrasts without discords, harmonies without monotony."

This happens to be the only bit of writing fresh from his first impressions of Venice. One would like to have found something that he had written when he first stood before the "Peter Martyr," Titian's great "Assumption," the "Miracle of St. Mark," or the "Colleoni"—all of these great works remembered by him as "amongst the greatest examples of art, reflecting all the splendour of the great republic." I recollect that the Accademia was at that time in a state of some confusion, and Mr. Kerr-Lawson tells me he remembers Mr. Watts saying that all the Carpaccios—which were unknown to him—were turned with their faces to the wall, and that he ventured to turn one partly round, exclaiming to Mr. Stanhope, "This is not bad!"

On their return journey they stopped at Padua for the purpose of seeing the work of Giotto in the cathedral. Of him he writes a few months later: "Giotto was a most wonderful man; departing from manner, dryness, and positive deformity, he displays beauty, dignity, and sweetness in degrees that perhaps have never been exceeded. There is a majesty of form and largeness of character that no artist since his time has ever produced with equal simplicity. Haydon remarks upon the really strange resemblance some of his heads bear to the heads of the frieze of the Parthenon, and concludes that he must at second-hand have received instruction from Pheidias. He supposes that some wandering artist had made him acquainted either with some fragments or some drawings from the Panathenaic procession; but in Giotto there is so little evidence of imitation, and all appears to be so much of a piece, that it is more likely his original and powerful mind enabled him to perceive and seize upon the noblest properties in nature; and indeed it would require a still larger compass of mind to avoid servile imitation and repetition of a beloved model, and there is no trace of the mannerism that would have been inevitable in the works of Giotto. Yet certainly the resemblance in principles of form, exhibited in his heads especially, to those of the best time of Greek art—the age of Pheidias—is little less than marvellous. There is in the cathedral at Padua, amongst other fine things by him, the figure of an angel seated in a boat, that for grandeur and style might have been the work of Pheidias himself. I have seen nothing so like in the whole range of art, the dry sculpturesque qualities rendering it to the superficial observer more like, by suggesting sculpture, but at the same time rendering it less like in fact; for Pheidias was eminently pictorial, stopping short exactly at that point where richness and flexibility merges into the florid. In this quality of luscious breadth and richness of surface, his style later comes out gloriously; for Giorgione and Titian are wonderfully Pheidian in texture of flesh and drapery. In the flesh, the same breadth and richness of general treatment, rendered firm and solid by the larger markings given with great determination. The form is less perfect, but the feeling is identical. The drapery is really exact in treatment, crumpled, folded in every direction, sitting close to the figure, because it has been worn. The direction of fold is given by the movement and play of muscle; it is never tortured to make out the form, never clumped into masses, in a mistaken notion of breadth. However voluminous and ample the drapery may be in the works of Pheidias, Giorgione, or Titian, the figure never seems smothered or loaded. The drapery of Raphael has been justly celebrated for its grandeur and simplicity, but excellent as it is, it looks academic and like new blanket by the side of the Greek and the Venetian. It is remarkable that this peculiar quality of ease, flexibility, and richness seems to have been entirely overlooked in the Parthenon fragments, if indeed they have not been regarded as defects, which perhaps is most probable. No sculptor has seemed to consider that the great master intentionally cut up his drapery; yet what profound knowledge of both nature and of his materials has he not displayed! He knew that large plain masses, in so solid a material, would necessarily tell with great effect upon the eye; therefore if he made his less interesting forms of drapery heavy and simple, he could not prevent them from having an undue effect. By cutting up the drapery with innumerable folds, he gave the idea of flexible material, covering, but not trammelling the wearer, worn for ornament and use; by flowing lines he gave grace, by difference of surface he suggested a different material, by many folds he took away the importance of the mass, leaving the head and limbs free and uninterfered with, simple, massive, and important.

"An advocate for the use of colour in sculpture, and believing that Pheidias employed it, I see in the general treatment reasons in favour of the contrary opinion, which I am surprised have never been remarked; for his method of suggesting difference of texture and colour in the drapery (by means of his chisel alone) would certainly go far to render colour unnecessary, and might be triumphantly appealed to as an argument that Pheidias did not use colour.

"It has been often said that Nature is always the same—the broadest and simplest principles taken into consideration; she is, but it cannot be denied that great modifications take place. The sun shining upon scarlet drapery produces an effect as splendid as ever it did in ancient Greece or Venice; and—allowing for the effect of sun and climate—the vagabond scantily-covered tramp is not very unlike the mendicant who asked alms of Alcibiades. The country boy, in his well-worn smock frock, will to this day treat you to Pheidian folds. But form and colour of flesh have certainly deteriorated. The well-dressed gentleman of 1854 can bear small resemblance to the exquisite of the time of

Pericles; the limbs, deprived, by the fashion of modern clothing, of freedom, and shut off from the action of sun and air, never acquire their natural development, texture, or colour. The junctures alone are fine in form and natural in character, because they have so much work to do, they are obliged to perfect themselves, and therefore nature's intentions cannot be thwarted."

Here the MS. ends—whether intended for publication or merely part of a letter there is nothing to show.

On his return to England he took up the work at Lincoln's Inn, painting there by arrangement, only during the spring and summer vacations, and unfortunately much interrupted, especially as years went on, by illness. He had proposed to himself to paint on this great wall —the space being forty-five feet wide and forty feet high—the design he afterwards named "Justice—A Hemicycle of Law-givers." Preferring to work without having made any cartoon, as he had done for the "St. George," he followed the practice adopted by him for the large picture of Alfred, and made drawings, sometimes on so small a scale that the whole composition went into half a sheet of notepaper; no study seems to have been larger than a medium-sized sheet of drawing-paper could carry, though many of the heads of the legislators were drawn or painted life-size, his friends being laid under contribution in some degree as models for the various types. At one time he thought of asking students of art, "anxious, like young soldiers, to prove themselves," to give him assistance in the work. He did not remember whether or not he ever applied for this, but was quite certain that he never had any help whatever, and he attacked the big work single-handed. To him the subject appeared to be a great one, bound up with the evolution of civilisation—"that evolution in which our religion takes its place," he explained—and it is noticeable that Moses in the central place is head and shoulders above all others; and not only this, but he alone amongst the law-givers has the uplifted head and face, as if listening to something higher than human argument—the "practical mystic" who receives his orders direct from Heaven. Mahomet also turns with something of the same action, but he looks towards Moses rather than to the Invisible. He is one of the four singled out with intention to stand somewhat apart; the others being Alfred, Charlemagne, and Justinian.

The plaster was always freshly laid the day before he worked upon any part, and as far as he was able, with the careful attention of Messrs. Winsor and Newton, the colours were carefully chosen with regard to permanency.

One of the most enduring pleasures remaining in his memories of this time was that, whilst he painted, the voices of the choristers reached him from the chapel, either during service or at practice ; the pure sound of the boys' voices, going and returning as it were, wound about the building from the unseen and distant ; and he liked to fancy that a choir of angels was singing to him while he worked.

CHAPTER VI

WE want the soldiers of art, not the fencing masters.
                                    G. F. WATTS, 1850.

CHAPTER VI

Now under the hospitable roof of Little Holland House went in and out an ebb and flow of various members of the family: some staying for days, some for weeks, and some for years, but all claiming Mr. Watts as one of its members. It thus became impossible for them to continue to call him "Mr. Watts." A name had to be found, and it was found for him by Mrs. Prinsep's youngest sister Sophie—Mrs. Dalrymple—the one who, to the end of his life, when writing to him, signed herself as "*Sorella.*" It was she who first called him Signor, the little word, half name, half title, that suited so well; for the many who liked to claim him especially could use it without feeling that it had the familiarity of a Christian name. They generally took the first step by saying "the Signor," and yet it seemed a suitably intimate little name, when used by the few who were most near to him.

It is not easy to explain why, but somehow his personality made people think of queer little names for him, in great variety—from the little girl who tried to bribe him, all her heart intent upon his doing something she particularly wanted, who looked up coaxingly and said, "Do, and I'll call you Fish"; to the full-grown girl who chose to call him "Lamb," mixing her metaphors when he was a little fussed about some unpunctuality one day, by saying, "Now, darling Lamb, don't be an old maid"—to which he replied, laughing, "Ah, you have none of the vices of old maids, nor the politeness of kings." "Early Lambs," she dubbed his first paintings.

But "Signor" was the universal name, and his own name George fell out of use entirely. In Mr. Harry Prinsep's mind remains a charming bit of vivid recollection of the godmother who gave Signor that name; and though he spoke of the years 1864-65, the reminiscence may take its place here. A nephew of Mr. Thoby Prinsep's, he was one of the family for whom Little Holland House was a home, and where for some two years between school and taking up his profession he lived and used to write for and read to his uncle, who was suffering from cataract. "Perhaps we were all round the dinner-table," he said, "in the lower dining-room—Uncle Thoby thinking about his work, passing his hand over his eyes and silent; Signor not very well and silent; Aunt Sara occupied giving all sorts of directions in a low tone to a servant; the young people awed and silent. Suddenly there was a rustle of silks, a lovely vision appeared—for Aunt Sophie wandered in, dressed in a gown of some rich colour, all full of crinkles" (the male mind describing marvellously drawn gathers and folds). "Aunt Sara would scold her a little for being late, and she would put her head on one side and answer with a little bit of pathetic humour; and before she had been amongst us three minutes, the whole party was laughing and talking."

With her head a little on one side, with down-dropped lids and red-brown hair, Signor has painted a miniature portrait of her on panel, in a green dress full of "crinkles," a string of coral beads about her neck. Years afterwards, on the back of that picture he wrote the words, "The days that are no more."

Mrs. Dalrymple's movements were beautiful, and the soft material she wore fell into arrangements of line full of suggestion to the artist's eye. To be always at hand, he carried in his pocket a small notebook of indelible paper with a metal point in the sheath, and when his eye fell on any particularly beautiful arrangement in posture or line he would call out, with a gesture of his hand, "Oh, pray, stay where you are for a moment," and the notebook was taken out to receive a monumental outline on the tiny page. These drawings, perhaps the least well known of his artistic expressions, may be placed, I venture to say, beside his greatest. They are chiefly drawn from Mrs. Prinsep, Lady Dalrymple, Mrs. Jackson and her three daughters Adeline, Julia, and Mary, who from their childhood were much

GEORGE FREDERIC WATTS

at Little Holland House. His larger drawings in chalk and charcoal are much better known. Several of these of the Prinsep family were to be seen on the walls of old Little Holland House, including that of Mr. Thoby Prinsep himself, his three sons, and one of Lady Somers. And with these were also the studies from Arthur as a boy, with the locks that the painter bribed him to keep uncut while he was making the drawings from which his pictures of "Sir Galahad," "Aspiration," "Hyperion," and of the "Red Cross Knight with Una," were afterwards painted. The full-face portrait of Arthur, reproduced in the picture "Aspiration," was borrowed by Mr. Holman Hunt when he was painting his famous picture of "Christ among the Doctors." He told Signor it was the type of head that he wished to keep in his mind when rendering this subject. By the time this picture was painted Arthur Prinsep had developed into the usual close-cropped schoolboy, and therefore never sat for this.

These drawings were not exhibited at the time that they were made; not that Sir Charles Eastlake did not appreciate them, but a rule in the Academy bye-laws at the time prevented any drawing that was merely a head from being shown there. Sir Henry Thoby Prinsep tells me that he remembers Sir Charles Eastlake coming, time after time, to try and persuade Signor to add just a few lines to outline the shoulders in each; but he would not, as he could not per-

Old Little Holland House from the North East

suade himself that it would add to the artistic worth.

As the attractions of Little Holland House gradually became more widely known, an unusually interesting society gathered there; especially on Sunday afternoons, when Mrs. Prinsep was "At Home" and Mr. Prinsep and Signor were known to be at leisure. Women remarkable for gifts of talent and beauty went there, as well as statesmen, soldiers, painters, poets, and men famous in literature. Thus under the cottage-like thatched porch many a distinguished head stooped and uncovered, to whom, figuratively, the world now pays that mark of reverence. So near London—though the sound of its traffic was not more than the sound of a distant river—the stately trees, and the wide green spaces merged on all sides in the acres of Holland House, were alone attractive enough to make the place popular. But when to this was added a hostess who, with a genius for hospitality, drew wit and beauty and talent together, the entertainment was irresistible.

In a letter to me from Lady Constance Leslie, she recalls her visit to Little Holland House. "It was in 1856, when we were first engaged to be married, that John took me to what was to me a new world—something I had never imagined before of beauty and kindness. I was a very ignorant little girl, and oh how proud I felt, though rather unworthy of what seemed holy ground. The Signor came out of his studio all spirit and so delicate, and received me very kindly as John's future wife. Thackeray was there with his young daughters, Coutts Lindsay, Jacob Omnium, and Lady Somers glorious and benevolent. Signor was the whole object of adoration and care in that house. He seemed to sanctify Little Holland House. I also remember well the Sunday, June 13, 1858, when we were dining with the Prinseps, Alfred Tennyson, Rossetti, Tom Taylor, Adelaide Sartoris, Edward Burne-Jones, Coutts Lindsay, and Richard Doyle. Adelaide Sartoris sang his own poems to Tennyson. In later years arose the vision of beauty, dear May Prinsep, and I remember seeing Val carry young Philip Burne-Jones upstairs—such a contrast! Val as St. Christopher!"

On weekdays the round of work went on—Mr. Prinsep at the India Office, the work in the studio rigorously uninterrupted. Signor's nature, his work, and his health all compelled him to live somewhat apart; though sympathy and vivid life were so essential to him that through life he almost craved for these, and drew them to him unfailingly. Amongst other friends of this time the author of *Tom Brown's School Days*, Mr. Tom Hughes, his brothers and their only sister Jeanie (Mrs. Nassau Senior), were much at Little Holland House. Being an only daughter, she had been brought up in her country home entirely with her brothers; her naturally bright and spontaneous out-of-door nature appealed to Signor greatly, and she soon became a friend-in-chief amongst many friends. To her care is owed the preservation of many sketches and designs, made while he was working out various ideas, and collected in two scrap-books at a time when they were littering his studio, which but for her forethought would certainly have disappeared. His health during these years was very uncertain; and the letters written to her seem to point to physical depression, and to confirm Mr. Valentine Prinsep's opinion that old Little Holland House did not suit Signor—the sanitation he declared was very far from satisfactory. Partly for change, and partly on the invitation of the Hollands, who were in Paris at the time, he spent some months of the winter of 1855–56 there, having a studio at 10 Rue des Saints Pères. He took with him Arthur Prinsep, a boy of fifteen, full of spirit and fun, and needing some handling. He tells me that Signor's curb upon him was simply, "Well, if you do that I shall have a headache"—an appeal to his affectionate nature much more effective than any command would have been, the boy knowing what real suffering the word headache could cover in Signor's case. It was here that M. Thiers came to sit to him, and one sentence of the conversation Signor remembered, because it seemed to him very typical of the Gallic mind, as distinct from the Anglo-Saxon. When talking of the Frenchman who had invented a statement that his fellow-countryman had anticipated Newton's great discovery of the law of gravitation, M. Thiers, though admitting that it was untrue, ended by saying, "Well, he had the glory of his country at heart, and I applaud this, and would like to put up a statue to his memory."

Prince Jerome Buonaparte, brother of the first Napoleon, also sat to him here; so did the Princess Lieven, whose husband had been from 1812 to 1834 the Russian Ambassador in England; the portrait happened to be painted during the last months of her life. Her letters to Metternich, and to her brother, Count Benckendorff, are well known. She was the friend of Lady Holland, to whom he gave the portrait. Of this time Mr. Nathaniel Hone kindly writes to me :—

"I was commencing my art studies, and I shall never forget Mr. Watts's kindness and the excellent advice he gave me. Some successful artists become vain and conceited; Watts had not those faults, he was most affable and kind to me as a student. We smoked many pipes together, discussing past and present art. I think among the ancients Titian was his favourite." "The many pipes smoked"—as far as one person was concerned—is a figure of speech, as Signor never smoked at any time of his life.

At the end of February he left Paris and returned to Little Holland House. During the months when he could not work at Lincoln's Inn, he had begun to fresco the dining-room of a house in Carlton House Terrace (No. 7), then belonging to Lord Somers; and this work he continued and probably completed during the spring and summer. The subjects he chose for these frescoes were the Elements, and to represent these he drew upon Greek mythological story. But he was constantly ill, and later in the same year, greatly urged by Dr. Gully, he accepted Charles Newton's invitation to join the staff of the expedition he was directing for the recovery of the Mausoleum of Halicarnassus at Budrum in Asia Minor.

He left England in the middle of October, in H.M.S. *Gorgon*, then under the command of Captain Towsey, with a crew of 150 men. He looked back upon this time—some eight months spent almost continuously upon a man-of-war, with great pleasure. He appreciated the order and discipline on board, made friends with both officers and men, and had a favourable outward journey till within sight of Malta, where for two days they tossed about, unable to enter the harbour—not a pleasant experience. At Smyrna they picked up Mr. Newton and went on to Budrum, where they got to work on the great excavations; Mr. Newton, an officer, and some sappers encamped on shore, while the staff remained on board. Christmas on the *Gorgon* was kept in English fashion, the sailors dancing and making merry. There was an impromptu concert in which Signor took part, and sang Dibdin's song "Tom Bowling" with such effect as to reduce the bluejackets to tears.

But Mr. Newton was above all things anxious to secure the lions' heads—Greek, and of the school of Scopas. He had the year before discovered these in the mediæval tower of St. Peter, built into its walls by the Knights Templars. A firman for this being necessary, he sent Signor on to Constantinople with despatches to Lord Stratford de Redcliffe, the British Ambassador, asking him to obtain the firman with all possible speed. Signor soon learnt, however, that speed was neither likely nor possible. Delay after delay occurred, but meantime he had a pleasant life at Constantinople, sometimes making acquaintance with the extortions of Misseri, the owner of the Hôtel d'Angleterre, more often on the man-of-war, a guest at the Embassy, or sometimes on board the *Royal Albert*, the flagship of Admiral Lord Lyons; and he was also sent for a cruise on board H.M.S. *Swallow* (Captain Maddiston) through the Greek islands and to Athens, a cruise he had permission from Lord Lyons to direct, who said playfully, "I put you in command." He never forgot the delight given him by the wonderful blueness of the waters seen through the port-holes at night, and often spoke of one night as more splendid than all others when he was dining on board the *Royal Albert*.

With Sir Henry Layard, in late years, he often talked over acquaintances and episodes of this time. Sir Henry was not with him there, but knew intimately Lord Stratford and all the staff of the Embassy at that time. Of Charles Alison —the many-sided and most remarkable of men— they often talked. He seemed to possess every talent, and a kind of mesmeric power over his chief and over most people whom he came across, and had much influence with the Turks. When Signor was at Constantinople, Mr. Alison was living in a tent in the Embassy garden, refusing, as a protest, to live under the roof of his impetuous chief.

Lord Stratford consented to sit for two portraits : one of these now in the National Portrait Gallery was unfinished and was completed many years later. When speaking generally of the confidences made to him by his sitters, Signor used to say that Lord Stratford was the most indiscreet of them all. Perhaps he knew best the loyalty of his painter. Meanwhile Mr. Newton was beginning to get desperate about the firman, and the wily Turks were at work, trying to possess themselves of the lions' heads ; indeed they were actually already in a caique on the morning when the *Swallow* appeared with the necessary firman. Mr. Newton secured them not a moment too soon. In excavating they would now and then find an absolutely perfect specimen of colour, but so evanescent that, in a few minutes of sunlight, it would utterly disappear. One instance of this Signor mentioned as almost unbelievably swift in its disappearance. A great block happened to be turned over while Mr. Newton was absent, and the workmen called Signor to see it. On it was a border of leaf and flower ornament in strong fine colour—red, yellows, and blues. He had the slab covered up as quickly as possible, but when turned round and uncovered again for Mr. Newton's inspection, the colour had utterly vanished.

He was much attracted by the men of the place. The dragoman, with his good looks and Eastern gift of good manners—"such a gentleman," as Signor used to say—sat to him for studies more than once. He was struck by the true spirit of the Mahommedan's interpretation of their prophet's teaching. For instance, as the habit of smoking was not of his time, it could not have been forbidden by him; nevertheless, during their fast of Ramadan the workmen never smoked from sunrise till sunset, and he watched them sitting with pipe filled and match in hand, waiting till the gun was fired as the sun dropped before they entered upon this delight. Later, an earnest convert to the Church of Rome happened to be sitting to him in Lent, and remarked, as he smoked, how glad he was that tobacco had not been discovered when the fast was instituted.

Towards the end of May, a man-of-war homeward bound took him, Val Prinsep, and Roddam Spencer Stanhope on board, and they set their faces homewards. Landing at Rhodes, they saw the pathetic sight of that town which shortly before had been shattered by a terrible earthquake. One single wall of a clock-tower stood alone, the hands pointing to the hour of the catastrophe. Still more impressive was the bowed figure of an old woman, who sat day after day on the summit of a high staircase still intact against an otherwise ruined wall, her head bent upon her knees, the very impersonation of ruin, loneliness, and despair; they were told she sat there constantly. The misery had been greatly enhanced by the apathy of the Turkish authorities, who did nothing to rescue, nor later to compensate in any way, the miserable remnant of the population.

It was June before they reached England. The visas on his passport are dated Smyrna, May 22, and Malta, May 26. On his way between these places, he writes to Mrs. Nassau Senior about the work of his brother-artists : " I long to hear what the exhibition will be, and shall expect to hear at Malta. Alas, I shall not be at home till long after the opening. I hope and trust Leighton has done his best and will thoroughly establish himself. I expect much from Hunt and also from Millais."

The news of the outbreak of the Indian Mutiny had not reached them at Malta; but on his return he found his friends at Little Holland House had been receiving disquieting news from India, where their eldest son, Henry, had gone, and where the youngest, Arthur, had but lately joined his regiment. The year that followed was naturally one of great tension. But the arts of peace, in spite of all the anxiety and trouble of that time, must needs be carried on, and his first care was to write as follows :—

"Little Holland House,
"Kensington,
"14th *June* 1857.

"Sir—I hasten to inform you that I have just returned to England, and am most anxious to recommence and carry out the work I have on hand at Lincoln's Inn, and which, unfortunately for myself and to the annoyance of the Benchers, has been so much interrupted. With the reason of the slowness of my progress, and the long interruption, the gentlemen forming that body must be acquainted, as I wrote to Mr. Hardwicke upon the subject, and my deplorable state of health was well known to many gentlemen connected with Lincoln's Inn. I have returned from a warm climate for the present at least much better, and whilst I am so, I desire to devote my whole time and energy to the prosecution of the fresco, and unless my health should break down again entirely, may reasonably hope to complete almost the whole of the picture before the winter sets in. If I were strong, I might bind myself by a positive engagement to finish it altogether by that time, but the work is laborious, and although my health is greatly improved, I have been so long and so very ill that I dare not hope it is yet perfectly restored. I beg to assure the Benchers that nothing but actual physical inability has prevented the vigorous progress of a work which I feel myself peculiarly bound by honour to use my utmost exertions to bring to a successful conclusion.—I have the honour to be your obedient servant, G. F. WATTS.

"SIR JOHN STUART."

On his return from these travels he found the Poet Laureate a guest at Little Holland House ; and Signor well remembered the grand figure, pacing up and down in the garden thinking over those lines in " Guinevere " where Arthur passes from her sight. He also remembered that the poet told him that at one time he had intended to use the character of Arthur as a figure to represent Conscience, but in working out the poem he had found himself unable to carry on this idea. Mrs. Tom Taylor was often at Little Holland House at this time, and had set to music the poem called " The Sisters." She sang the words so dramatically that at the line,

Three times I stabbed him thro' and thro'.

the poet turned to Signor, and said in his deep voice, " And she would have done it too." It was now, or very soon after this, that the first portrait of Tennyson was painted, not that which is so well known, and which at the time it was painted was called " the great moonlight portrait," the one which is in the possession of Lady Henry Somerset. The first portrait is now in the Melbourne Gallery, the head is seen in profile; it was painted in 1857, the other in 1858–59. While this last portrait was being painted, the Laureate, who was then writing the idyll, "Elaine, the Fair Maid of Astolat," asked Signor what was in his mind when he set to work upon a portrait, and the words of his reply, having passed through the mind of the poet, lie embedded in the poem. It was at this time that another life-long friend came to Little Holland House. In the *Memorials* of her husband by Lady Burne-Jones, she quotes from a note of his: "One day Gabriel took me out in a cab—it was a day he was rich, so we went in a hansom, and we drove and drove until I thought we should arrive at the setting sun—and he said, 'You must know these people, Ned; you will see a painter there—paints a queer sort of pictures, about God and Creation.' So it was he took me to Little Holland House."

Signor had known Rossetti for some time, Millais and Holman Hunt longer; but with Mr. Burne-Jones only now began the long friendship. A year later, when Mr. Burne-Jones was staying at Little Holland House, the Poet Laureate, also staying there, overheard Ruskin in another room exclaim, "Jones, you are gigantic," and the Laureate dubbed him "Gigantic Jones." At this same time Signor writes to Mrs. Nassau Senior: "With regard to the painted window, there is at this moment—

staying at Little Holland House with Val—the very man you want, Jones by name—a real genius! really a genius!"—the apostrophes probably referring to his having already spoken to her too often, perhaps in superlatives, of all that was good in the work of other painters. It was indeed a gift of his nature to find out excellencies, and to avoid seeing failure; although the gift was not needed in this case, where the real genius had existed and been attested. But its possession was well known to his friend "Ned Jones," who once said, "Signor admires paintings that would make very good soles for his boots!" I remember repeating to my husband a remark of Mr. Du Maurier's on the lenient view he always took of the foibles and faults of human nature; alas, I cannot now recall the humorous saying at which Signor laughed heartily, and said, "Any affection that has been given to me, I am sure is due to the fact that it is difficult for me not to see the best in people. I think I am not deceived, but their good qualities are uppermost to me."

It was in July that Rossetti and Burne-Jones began their work of painting on the walls of the Oxford Union, having drawn upon Little Holland House for the help of two young painters, Roddam Spencer Stanhope and Val Prinsep, who joined them a few weeks later. In a letter to his old friend Lady Duff Gordon, Signor mentions his share in persuading Mr. Prinsep to take up this work: "I daresay even in Rome you think of India in the morning and of India at night, as we do here. Never were expectations more signally disappointed than those of universal peace that were so confidently indulged in in 1851. Mrs. Prinsep has been in great agony of mind about her two sons in India, but thank God they are, or were by the last news, safe, though they have both run fearful risks. I daresay you know that the second son has taken up the arts as a profession. I have conscientiously abstained from inoculating him with any of my views or ways of thinking, and have plunged him into the Pre-Raphaelite Styx. I don't mean to say that I held the fine young baby of six feet two by the heel, or wish to imply the power of moulding his opinions at my pleasure; but, to continue my figure, I found him loitering on the banks and gave him a good shove, and now his gods are Rossetti, Hunt, and Millais—to whose elbows more power. The said Master Val—commonly called Buzz by reason of his hair, which is this sort of thing

[Here follows a scribble of the bristling hair.]

—has made most satisfactory progress, and has distinguished himself by painting a picture at Oxford fourteen feet long with figures ten feet high—'A muffin!'"

Later Signor, becoming somewhat anxious about the effect that this dominance of Rossetti's mind was having over the mind of "the fine young baby," wrote to Mr. Ruskin about it, feeling truly that the mediævalism natural to Rossetti was but a mere reflection in the younger mind, not his own natural expression. Upon this Mr. Ruskin writes (Oct. 18, 1858):—

"I was very glad to have your letter, entirely feeling with you in this matter, and even more culpable than you charge me with being," and admitting that he had encouraged the stiffness and quaintness and intensity as opposed to classical grace and tranquillity, adds, "Now I am suffering for so yielding to my own likings, all the more that I have been having a great go with Paul Veronese. I was six weeks at Turin, working from a single picture of his, a bit here and a bit there: came to great grief, of course, but I learned a great deal: more than I ever learned in six weeks, or six months, before. I will try to get hold of Val this week and have a serious talk with him. I see well enough there's plenty of stuff in him, but the worst of it is that all the fun of these fellows goes straight into their work, one can't get them to be quiet at it, or resist a fancy; if it strikes them ever so little a stroke on the bells of their soul, away they go to jingle, jingle, without ever caring what o'clock it is. When can I see *you*? Sincere regards to Mrs. Prinsep.—Always yours affectionately, J. RUSKIN."

To the Exhibition at the Academy of 1858, after being absent as an exhibitor for five years, he sent a portrait head of Miss Mabel Eden, and two full-length portraits, one of Miss Senior and the other of her sister-in-law, Mrs. Nassau Senior, all three painted during the last nine months. Signor was now occasionally using copal varnish as a medium, the result of talking over the advantages of various mediums with Rossetti, Millais, and perhaps Ruskin. Being at this time at work upon walls, not only at Lincoln's Inn, but at Carlton House Terrace and at Bowood, he was, in his portraits, using the utmost care—sometimes even hatching with fine strokes of the brush in the underpainting—to counterbalance the effect of the work which, as a whole, was of necessity broad and less precise. His own inclination was for matt surfaces and crisp dry touches, and the use of varnish as a medium was really disagreeable to him. I have heard him and Val Prinsep have a passage-at-arms upon the subject, Mr. Prinsep maintaining that under Rossetti's influence Signor had for some years painted all his pictures with copal varnish, which he in his turn most stoutly denied. The portrait of Mrs. Nassau Senior, one of Mrs. George Cavendish-Bentinck and her children, and the portrait of Miss Alice Prinsep at the piano were painted with copal; but on beginning a portrait of Lady Somers, which in the general scheme of colour and treatment greatly resembles this last-mentioned portrait, and is of the same date, he made use of benzoline; and finding that when he tried to take out a certain part of the background the paint used with this medium had become so hard that nothing would touch it, he continued to use benzoline until later, when the chemists, Messrs. John Bell and Co., provided him with a preparation of petroleum, called by them rock oil. This, suiting him even better, was the medium he used to the end, the smallest possible quantity of linseed oil being added to diminish the volatile quality of the petroleum. While the portrait of Mrs. Nassau Senior is brilliant in colour, and as delicate in handling as a miniature, Miss Senior's is much broader in treatment and richer in the *impasto* quality of its surface.

He wished to avoid enthralment by any fixed method, and therefore approached different subjects, each with the technique he thought the most suitable. In various parts of a drawing he would point out where he had purposely varied the character of line. He considered it unintellectual not to do this. No compliment gave him such pleasure as to be told, by any one looking at his work, that they would not have known that the picture was by his hand. "I don't endeavour to be different," he said, "but taking a different class of subject, the treatment naturally becomes different. If I tried to make it so purposely, I should most likely get into a mess."

Owing to a sort of curiosity to see whether his manner was recognisable or not, he exhibited three pictures at the Academy Exhibition this year (1858) under the name of F. W. George.

The secret was in fact no secret; for if his sitters had been bound over to silence the subject of his portraits would have betrayed it, for they were ladies with large acquaintances, and he was well known as a great friend of theirs.

This year Signor painted the portrait on panel of Mr. Gladstone, now in the National Portrait Gallery; and at this time he used occasionally to go to the breakfasts given by Mr. and Mrs. Gladstone, as he had some years before gone to those given by Samuel Rogers.

The big fresco had now been carried well forward during the spring and autumn vacations, and Sir Henry Taylor, having been allowed to see it, had written in warm praise of the work. From Sandown House, Esher, on September 18, 1859, Signor replies:—

"I am somewhat late in returning my acknowledgment to you for your letter, because I am very much occupied by my fresco, and writing costs me at all times an effort I am but too much inclined to defer. A thousand thanks, for I know that you intended me gratification. I neither affect nor desire to be indifferent to praise, for it would be no advantage to arrive at that unsympathetic state which could render one careless about sympathy. Criticism is indeed unpalatable to me, as it can only tell me what I so well know already, and do not require to be told, as I would remedy that matter if I could.

"I have plenty of ambition and ardently desire to be useful in my generation, but I would prefer working silently and unnoticed, save by that amount of encouragement that would cheer my efforts when well directed, and for the sake of their direction alone ; to produce great things one ought to be intent only upon doing one's utmost, and never stop to consider whether the thing be great or little in the abstract. The really great is so far beyond one's reach that comparison becomes an unworthy consideration ; to work with all one's heart, but with all singleness of heart, is the right thing, and whoso does this may feel satisfied, whatever the result of his labour may be. I, in this instance, would feel satisfied if I had been able to do my best ; but many circumstances, want of health foremost amongst them, have prevented me from doing my best, so I cannot be contented. The utmost I can hope is that my work will not be a disgrace, and my hope is founded upon a steady rejection of small effects. If I have shown the way to better things, I shall be very well contented, but I neither expect nor desire that my work may be considered a great one.

" Mrs. Cameron's enthusiastic and extravagant admiration is really painful to me, for I feel as if I were practising a deception upon her. She describes a great picture, but it is hers and not mine. Saying so much upon the subject will probably look very much like vanity, and I confess that I feel conscious of some worth which I do like to be estimated justly ; but my pride is more hurt by over-estimation than by want of appreciation,—and I am really humiliated by praise which is only due to perfect success."

In October 1859 he writes to Mrs. Nassau Senior :—

"I have this day put the last touches in my fresco at Lincoln's Inn! I dare not call it finished, but it must go. I feel sad at giving it up, for now I cannot cheat myself any longer with the belief that I am going to improve it ; alas, for the failure, as it is, for I shall never again have so fine a space. I don't mean to say that it is a disgraceful or a mean failure, but it is a failure ; and the only consolation I have is in the very strong feeling I have that I can do much better." And to the architect of the Hall he sent the following letter :—

"Little Holland House,
"Kensington, W.
"*October* 17*th*, 1859.

"Dear Sir—I beg to announce to you and to the Benchers of Lincoln's Inn that I have completed the fresco in the Hall, and to thank the gentlemen composing the Honourable Society for their patience and consideration. It has been with great vexation to myself that their patience has been tried by the delay caused by my want of health.

"I will say nothing about my work excepting that I sincerely wish it were better. I do not expect that it will be popular, but I hope and think it will improve upon acquaintance.

GEORGE FREDERIC WATTS

"I have preferred to leave it a pure fresco—'Buon Fresco'—instead of retouching it with distemper colour, the effect of real fresco being nobler, and the work more permanent (careful washing will not injure it).

"I beg to be allowed to suggest that the long window on the south-west side should have stained glass put in throughout; it would harmonise better with the opposite window, and though it would in a slight degree diminish the light, the picture would lose nothing, my object being dignity and monumental solemnity.

"Fresco also, unlike every other method of painting, lights up the space it occupies, which is one of its great advantages over every other kind of painting applied to the purpose of mural decoration.

"I have the honour to be your obedient servant, G. F. WATTS."

The fresco was warmly approved by many of his friends, amongst them Dante Gabriel Rossetti, who, writing to Mr. Bruce (afterwards Lord Aberdare), says: "I have indeed seen Watts's fresco and think it by far the finest specimen of the method we have seen among modern ones. The foreground figures and those of the second plane are especially admirable, and do not betray in the least the trammels of fresco. No doubt Watts has overcome the difficulties of his task in the only possible way, that is, by risking much, painting fearlessly, and removing part when necessary. The advance in power from the background parts, painted first, to the foreground ones, is most refreshing. It is a very good work indeed, taken altogether, and does honour to the country."

To Mrs. Dalrymple he also writes: "Let me add a word to tell you how I smuggled myself in at last (hoping, however, that friends were no longer contraband) to see that great work of Watts's. From what I have heard of its progress he must have done wonders at the last, in almost no time. And certainly the last parts must be as fine as any fresco to be seen anywhere; they are far finer than any I ever saw. How one must feel that one may rest a little after finishing such a work, yet how one must long to begin again. Will it ever be my lot, I wonder, to earn such a double sensation! It is the only thing to hope for in the world. Will you give the Signor my share of the thanks that every one owes him?"

The *Times* had a most appreciative article on this fresco, and published a day or two later a letter from a friend, Sir Henry Layard, his principal object in writing being "to express a hope that when the day is longer, and the sun brighter, the Benchers of Lincoln's Inn will open this noble hall for a short time to the public at large." "I have read," the letter continues, "with much gratification the remarks in the *Times* of yesterday on Mr. Watts's noble fresco in the new Hall of Lincoln's Inn. I had previously seen but one notice of that remarkable work, and had read it with sincere pain. Whatever there may be in the fresco deserving of criticism—and what human work is without fault?—no man of feeling or of knowledge could approach without reverence, or describe without deep respect for its author, this great effort of a man of undoubted genius, the result of some years of earnest labour and study, carried on in spite of the disadvantage of ill-health and want of sympathy, and executed without other reward than that which his ardent love of art could afford.

"In Raphael's frescoes in the Vatican an angel may be detected with three legs and an apostle with six fingers, but what should we think of the man who, after contemplating those immortal works, could leave them without any other impression than the satisfaction afforded by the discovery of such blemishes? I am one of those who have long hoped to see painting again employed, as it was during the Middle Ages, on truly great and National subjects, and worthily exercising its best and highest mission among us. I have consequently watched, as others have done, with interest and anxiety the progress of the fresco upon which Mr. Watts has been employed for the last five years in Lincoln's Inn. The result has far exceeded my expectation; we have at last one great work worthy of the country. I trust that it may lead to the introduction of a class of painting which will place the English school in the first rank, and will restore to this branch of the Fine Arts its highest and most legitimate function. An intimate acquaintance with, I believe, every fresco of importance of the great painters in Italy, and with most of the attempts at mural decoration that have been made of late to the north of the Alps, leads me to assert without hesitation, although it is sometimes dangerous to pronounce dogmatically on matters of art, that there has been no such fresco painted since the best period of Italian art, whether as regards mastery over the material, breadth and truth of conception, right understanding of the noblest end of painting, or philosophic treatment. I will even venture to say that the upper line of seated figures will bear comparison with the greatest works of the old masters, and I entirely agree with your remark that had this fresco been anywhere else but in England, it would have become to us 'an object of reverent pilgrimage.'

"That we shall sooner or later appreciate it, and that it will ultimately exercise that influence upon English art which such a work ought to exercise, I cannot doubt."

When answering a letter which had expressed pleasure in this work, the painter says: "I am much gratified by your expressions of approval of my fresco, and hope you will not find cause to change your opinion.

"I think the only explanation I can attempt

will be limited to naming the figures; the picture cannot be said to have a subject, being neither historical, nor allegorical, nor poetical, and aiming at no dramatic expression or effect; I would call it suggestive, my intention being to produce a combination of forms and colour which should have a grand monumental effect, and pervade, so to speak, the building like a strain of Handel's music, becoming one with the architecture. This may seem too fanciful and vague to such as look upon art only as a means of illustrating actual events, or interesting by direct and exact imitation; but I think, if I have opportunities, I shall be able to prove that the principle is well worth working out. I should wish to see painted round the Hall a series of pictures representing such historical events as have reference to the development of law in England, painted with historical exactness. In accordance with this principle I have avoided disturbing the flat surface of the wall by much perspective or projection, endeavouring to give my figures solidity rather than relief, general power rather than individuality, the region being altogether different from domestic or dramatic art; feeling that to attempt anything like illusion, to stick real men and women upon a wall, would vulgarise, even though it might increase the effect. For the same reason I have avoided high lights, even on the faces; and indeed have made no more of the heads than of other parts, keeping the uniformity of tone which figures have when seen from a distance.

"Knowing the interest you take in the subject, I intrude these remarks upon you because I would anticipate certain criticisms which I know will be made, and I wish to account for some things which will be considered objections, and to separate intentional results from defects arising out of inability to do better.

"Perhaps you may sometimes discuss the subject of mural decoration. At the risk of being tedious, I will repeat that I am convinced we shall never have really great art in England, or have the capabilities of English art fairly tested, until wall-painting becomes habitually practised; until artists know by experience that the general treatment of a design must be varied, according to the conditions under which he works.

"At present the Royal Academy Exhibition supplies a universal test which is in reality only applicable to exhibition pictures. The noblest art ever has been and ever must be connected and almost identified with architecture, and the effects of oil-painting, beautiful as they are, will never harmonise with architectural effects. I have some hope that the Benchers of Lincoln's Inn, having taken up the subject of mural decoration by giving me the opportunity of painting so large a space, will think over the design I had in view with regard to the complete decoration of the Hall (at a convenient height from the floor), subjects from the history of England. It appears to me that this is exactly the sort of thing the Royal Academy ought to undertake, by supplying designs to be worked out by competent students, under the supervision and with the instruction of professors; the experience gained, if these courses of study were pursued, being exactly what created great artists formerly. To these, paintings by fresco would be a prelude, or introductory chapter."

The painter was entertained to dinner by the Benchers on April 25, 1860, " an honour," the *Times* remarks, " before conferred on no other painter except Hogarth, who dined there in the year 1750." Mr. Watts was presented by the Society with a cup of the value of £150 and a purse containing £500, " the testimonial," so the address explained, " being not in the character of compensation, but as a testimonial of the friendly feeling of the Society for the man who had selected it as the recipient of so valued a gift, and of its appreciation of his genius as an artist."

During the winters of the late 'fifties and early 'sixties, it became the habit of the family at Little Holland House to migrate to Esher, staying there several months during the worst part of the year. A widowed sister of Mr. Prinsep's, Mrs. Sandeman, invited them to do this, as she felt her loneliness; and Sandown House was capacious. Glad to escape the damp of winter and the fogs, Signor was generally of the party. Here he was able to enjoy hunting, sometimes with the Surrey Union Foxhounds, but more often with the Duc d'Aumale's Harriers. In a letter from Tom Taylor I find he says: "Thoby tells me you are doing nothing but laying in a stock of health and fresh air for the coming year's work." He baits an invitation to their house, within riding distance of Esher, by telling him that Mrs. Tom Taylor has "a newly dug-up composition of Beethoven's to play to you, the loveliest bridal chorus and maiden's magic from some long-forgotten melodrama called 'King Stephen of Hungary.'"

Beethoven was also being interpreted for him by a young German lady, who, in writing later to him, says that she found she could play her favourite master better to him and to Mrs. Tennyson and Sir Henry Layard than to any others.

The winters at Esher were good for him. The nearest approach to the understanding of the *joie de vivre* was when he had a good mount, and hounds were running. Riding to him was a fine art, and his groom was not allowed to exercise his horse on a snaffle-bit, his opinion being that by the use of this would-be humane bit the mouth of the horse was hardened, and the rider's hand became heavy. He condemned it as a practice which had never obtained amongst the nations habitually accustomed to be on horseback. He was much opposed to the docking of horses, and also to the bearing-rein, and published letters upon both these subjects.

Of the former he wrote : " The brutal fashion of docking horses is a disgrace to our civilisation, and cannot be too strongly protested against. With regard to the artistic side, there is a degraded want of taste in destroying the harmonious balance of nature's arrangement, the somewhat heavy head of the beautiful animal being balanced by the tail, which naturally should have considerable volume. Setting aside the disgusting cruelty, this want of taste, which can prefer to see the noble creature changed by the destruction of the fine appendage into a thing that resembles the stump of a worn-out broom —made to resemble a pig or a tapir—is very lamentable, when found among the classes that can boast of education and refinement. The cruelty is barbarous in those who practise it, infinitely degrading in those who encourage it from so mean a motive as fashion—only not contemptible because so much worse. I do not see how the Legislature or the Church can be indifferent to it. Cropping dogs' ears was, I believe, put down by law—docking is far worse ; indeed it is, I think, more degrading than bull-fighting. There is in that courage and address, though in a bad cause ; for the brutal practice of docking, a mere caprice of fashion, nothing can possibly be said—indeed, the short agony in the time of excitement is probably less than that suffered by the horse during the protracted time between the brutal (I wish I could find a stronger word) operation and the healing of it." And, as Signor pointed out, the suffering does not end with healing. To their latest years these unfortunate animals, when turned out in fields, are deprived of their natural protection against the stings of gnats and flies. In the hunting-field, the tail should act as a rudder.

He had once been able to teach a young lady[1] the art of a light hand. She had said to him despairingly, "I can never ride well—my brother tells me my heavy hand will always prevent this," and he undertook that if she came to ride in the paddock at Little Holland House, he would show her how to cure this fault, and he did so in two or three lessons. His love and his understanding of a horse was akin to that which is more commonly given to dogs; and in his art he liked to use the horse as a symbol as much as he liked to use the little child. "The horse worships too," some one has said in writing of the picture of Sir Galahad; and if carefully considered, I think it would be granted that the horse, wherever it is to be found in his work, is made to express an emotion almost human. His love of riding was a bond between him and many delightful friends at Esher, amongst them the French princes of the Orleans family, who were living then at Claremont and Twickenham. He saw much of them, and there are many friendly notes and letters from the two brothers,

---

[1] Miss Probyn, sister of Sir Dighton Probyn.

the Prince de Joinville and Duc d'Aumale, and their nephew the Duc de Chartres.

In the first of these, the Prince de Joinville asks permission for a party from Claremont and Twickenham to visit Lincoln's Inn, where the fresco had just been completed: another consults him about a drawing-master for his daughter, and Signor having recommended a Mr. Morelli for this post, the prince at first gratefully accepted the recommendation, and afterwards sent in hot haste to make all inquiries as to this man's political views. At the same time he explained that Panizzi had once recommended as a teacher an Italian, with whom all arrangements had been made, and the week following he was to have been at Claremont; however, they heard from him that he had suddenly been called on urgent business to Paris, and was therefore unable to present himself at Claremont. That man was Orsini, and his mission to Paris was the assassination of Napoleon Third. "History would never have cleared us had Orsini ever set foot in Claremont," and, the prince continued, "you may suppose we are careful now." A note from the Duc d'Aumale, though written some years later from Worcestershire, is characteristic of the prince's friendly regard.

"17*th Dec.*, 1862.

"CHER MONSIEUR WATTS—Aimez vous toujours l'air de la campagne and a good ride across country ? Si cela est, vous conviendrait-il de partir de Paddington le 26 à 1.5 P.M., d'amener votre cheval avec vous, de vous arrêter à la Station d'Evesham, et de venir achever le mois et l'année dans ce cottage au fond d'un bois ? Nous vous monterons des lièvres qui valent mieux que ceux du Surrey, et des fermiers hospitaliers et bons vivants qui ont conservé les traditions des vieux Yeomen. Au cottage, la vie de Campagne la plus simple, telle que vous l'aimiez je crois, et des gens qui seront charmés de vous avoir quelques jours sous leur toit.—Votre bien affectionné   H. D'ORLÉANS."

Society at Esher was in those years fortunate in having some residents to whose houses came people of whom Carlyle might have said, "They look beyond eating their pudding." One of these was the home of Sir Alexander Duff Gordon[1] and his wife Lucie, talented and beautiful, one whose charm won for her troops of friends; and with them was their daughter Janet, still in the schoolroom, but nevertheless a personage whether in the hunting-field or elsewhere. Then the Prinseps attracted their friends, and George Meredith his; for he was living at Copsham at this time, and it was now that the great novelist met Mrs. Norton,[2] though —as he once told me—only twice, and studied her as a type for Diana of the Crossways chiefly

[1] The son of his friend at Careggi. Their daughter Janet (Mrs. Henry Ross), now as well known as hostess of the villa Poggio Gherardo at Florence, and authoress.
[2] Daughter of Thomas Sheridan (1808-77), married the Hon. George Chapple Norton.

through the mind of her friend, Lady Duff Gordon. The chief incident, however, in the life of Diana was never suggested by this loyal friend, who always refused to listen to anything of the nature of scandal connected with Mrs. Norton's name, and indeed the incident was acknowledged to be pure fiction by the novelist himself. I heard Mr. Meredith and my husband talk over these memories. The grand flexibility of her beautiful nostril had struck them both. Diana is described as having the nostril of a war-horse; and Signor told him that when painting Mrs. Norton sometime before the Esher days— I believe at Holland House—he kept in his mind the thought of a grand old hunter, alert at hearing from a distance the running of hounds. In speaking of the extraordinary charm of Mrs. Norton's personality, Signor told me that no Diana, or any other heroine of romance, could represent her indescribable fascination. He had frequently met her at Holland House, and there also he had first made the acquaintance with the French princes.

During the winter of 1859 Lord and Lady Holland were at their villa in Naples, and there in December he died. Thus when Lady Holland returned again to England it was as the widowed mistress of Holland House, and Signor had suffered an irreparable loss.

CHAPTER VII

I WANT to make art the servant of religion by stimulating thought high and noble. I want to assert for art a yet higher place than it has hitherto had.

G. F. WATTS.

CHAPTER VII

THE first fresco at Bowood, painted in 1858, the subject being Achilles watching Briseis led away from his tents, seems to have been painted in a few weeks' time. The artist worked some twelve hours in the day if the weather prevented him from getting out for a canter over the Wiltshire Downs. On this first visit Lord Lansdowne, not being at Bowood, had begged him to take his own horse—his dear Undine—with him. The second fresco was delayed till July 1860 for reasons which he explains to Lady Somers. " In consequence of the want of health you are well acquainted with, and the heavy undertaking I had on hand at Lincoln's Inn, which I was under the necessity of completing, my affairs had become a good deal involved. I had some hard knots to untie, being positively obliged to paint some portraits in order to be able to pay my debts, or I might have—should have—been at work for Lord Lansdowne in the summer. I do confidently hope to paint the fresco in the spring. I have great difficulty in working out the subject; it is not a good one. It is impossible to invest the figure of Coriolanus with dignity, for indecision is not noble, and the shape of the space does not lend itself to picturesque general treatment, which might compensate for want of grandeur; but I must get over it as best I may. As for every reason it is important that the fresco should be begun and finished without any break, it is work that must be done during long and light days. In addition to the difficulty arising from short days in winter, the cold and varying temperature would be fatal to the drying and permanence of the colours and plaster. . . . I will write to Lord Lansdowne: no one can honour him more than I do, and no one's good opinion should I value more."

Letters from Lord Lansdowne show that the Coriolanus fresco was begun at the end of July, and in September final touches to both frescoes were all that remained to be done. As Signor certainly always spoke of the Lincoln's Inn fresco as the only true fresco in England, it is doubtful whether these two paintings were in "buon fresco." I am told that the frescoes look faded. If they have lost colour, they could not have been painted in pure fresco.

It was at this time, when the country was aroused by the general fear of invasion, that the magnificent Volunteer movement suddenly sprang into existence. Within the space of a few months a hundred thousand men had proved themselves willing and able to offer military service to their country, without coming upon the Government for the smallest fraction of the cost of equipment or training. It need hardly be said that this spirit was in accord with all Signor's ideas of patriotism, and he was himself soon enrolled as a member of the Artists' Corps —the spirit at least being more than willing. Almost simultaneously the movement to encourage the practice of rifle-shooting was set on foot, and with both these he was glad to be identified. I find a note from Lord Elcho, who had just then raised the London Scottish Volunteers.

"St. James's Place,
"Jan. 14th, 1860.

"My dear Watts—I wish to leave the conception as well as the drawing of our shield entirely to yourself. Our association calls itself the National Rifle Association. Our object is to encourage Volunteers and to nationalise rifle shooting, by establishing a Grand National Annual Meeting, where prizes will be shot for, first by Volunteers, secondly by all comers. If you could let me have a rough sketch of your idea of a shield for us, by Thursday morning, as we have a Committee Meeting at twelve, I should feel grateful. I hope you are getting strong. Can I help you in getting more wall space?—Yours sincerely, Elcho."

In a letter recently received by me (June

1912) from Lord Wemyss, he says of the shield: "Its shape was designed by a son of Mr. Cayley, M.P. for some Yorkshire constituency. Your dear husband said to me, 'Let it be made in iron, and six feet high.' On this basis we worked, I suggesting the subjects, and he drawing them as they seemed fittest for the shield. The work was entrusted to Elkington, the silversmiths, and the execution was by them given to a Belgium or Frenchman—'Mainfroid' by name; and when you think that it was *repoussé* out of a solid bit of iron plate, one's admiration is lost in wonder."

The figures on the shield were drawn by Signor, but not the surrounding decoration. It was at his suggestion that the target known as "the running man" became part of the Wimbledon programme for the National Rifle Association.

In the spring of 1855, friends writing from Rome had begged Signor to go to Bryanston Square to make the acquaintance of "a delightful young painter" who had just arrived there to pay a short visit to his father. The young painter had brought over his picture "Cimabue's Madonna" for exhibition at that year's Academy, and the name of Frederic Leighton was becoming known in London. "Forty years of unbroken friendship" were the last words written to lay at the feet of him whose acquaintance he now sought. In spite of a difference in age of some thirteen years, and perhaps because of a

GEORGE FREDERIC WATTS

still greater difference in the two characters, the bond between them became a strong one : each seemed to find in the other that which he would above all things have liked to find in himself. Leighton once said to a friend, " Don't envy me, envy Signor " ; while he, sketching out Leighton's admirable qualities and his own deficiencies as he was wont to do, remarked, " Nature got tired when she was in the middle of making me, left off, and went away and made a Leighton." A note now lying before me seems characteristic enough to quote :—

"2 ORME SQUARE,
"*Saturday.*
(Addressed to Esher ; Postmark, *Feb.* 18, 1861.)

" DEAR SIGNOR—Your letter has been duly forwarded to Mr. Barlow (Thomas O.), who lives at Auburn Lodge, St. Albans Road, Victoria Road, Kensington. I shall be charmed to hear of the dodges you have been devising in your rural retreat. Of course you will practically modify the method we talked over the other day—no artist with the stamp of his own can adopt unchanged the procedure of another— different results require different means. The happy years in which one believed implicitly in panaceas are no longer ours, I am afraid, my dear Signor ; those days of enviable intolerant convictions don't reach much beyond our teens. I hope when you come to town we may rub our brains together, to our mutual benefit—certainly to mine.—Many things to Mr. and Mrs. Prinsep, and to Alice, from, dear Signor, yours very truly, F. LEIGHTON."

It was a singular friendship, quite without undue interdependence. If Sir Frederic could have influenced Signor, there is no doubt that he would have dissuaded him from painting the class of subject which he (Signor) called "ethical reflections"; those pictures which Signor himself regarded as alone worthy to bequeath to public galleries.

On the other hand, Signor would fain have persuaded Sir Frederic to retain more of the beauty of his sketches in the finished work.

After Leighton had built his house in Holland Park Road, attracted to that part by the friends at Little Holland House, scarcely a day passed without a meeting between the two brothers-in-art; and young people coming home from their balls in London would often come across Leighton running in, soon after dawn, to have a few words with Signor before the day's work began.

In Mr. Harry Prinsep's vivid recollection of this time, this studio was singular for its simplicity: its floor covered with rough cocoanut matting, with only the simplest furniture, rich only in its "strange pictures of God and Creation," and to him in the beloved presence of Signor. He recollects how the door would fly open, and Leighton would appear running in as if finishing a two-mile race, and begin talking eagerly of a thousand things, his handsome mobile countenance lighted up with enthusiasm on one subject or another. "And I, only a chit of a boy, would receive every bit as much consideration from him as Signor did."

The "chit of a boy" was very dear to Signor, who after the separation of almost half a century still often regretted that his fate had taken him to the antipodes. They never met again.

Harry Prinsep could also give a vivid account of the first evening on which Joachim played at Little Holland House. It was after dinner in that drawing-room of harmonious colour, under the deep-blue ceiling, and Joachim leaning back had sunk into one of the biggest of sofas, when Signor ventured to ask him to play. Just at this time he and Harry Prinsep had both been impressed with the idea that they must learn to play the violin.[1] Signor had bought one for some twenty-five pounds, and Harry one for twenty-five shillings; and for the moment their great wish was to accomplish playing the melody of Beethoven's song "Adelaide." It was this song that Joachim was asked to play; he rolled that leonine head of his, and answered, "Why, yes, if you have a violin," upon which the boy sprang to his feet with delight, and ran to fetch his own. Joachim took it up, and still almost

---

[1] Signor continued to study this art for some years, but finding that he could not get beyond the point of having merely learnt his lesson, he became discouraged, and finally gave up the attempt. He explained to me that the whole difference lay between the execution which conveyed the sense of acquirement (with which he could not be satisfied) and the execution when the music seems to be the creation of the interpreter.

lying back, his left arm thrown up, and the violin held upright in the air, he drew the bow across the strings once or twice with a very dubious expression; then Signor intervened, saying, "There is one in my studio which is rather better," and it was sent for. "Ah! this will do," Joachim allowed, upon the second trial; and then away he went, drawing from the violin all that was possible, and making the room fill with the wonder of the song—an evening to remember; and the old twenty-five shilling violin, across the strings of which the master once drew the bow, is still intact, thousands of miles away from England, with a big "J" scratched upon it.

"A Lamplight Study—the Portrait of Joseph Joachim," will preserve for future generations his aspect on these evenings. In imagination one can see him standing, bow in hand and chin upon the violin, in that room with its wealth and colour from floor to ceiling, the art upon its walls answering so nobly to the music. Hallé at the piano, Joachim with eyes that seemed only to hear, not to see, the lamplight falling softly on the faces of beautiful women—probably Mrs. Sartoris (Adelaide Kemble), possibly Miss Emma Brandling,[1] Mrs. Norton, Lady Somers; Leighton was almost always there, perhaps Herschel and Browning, and besides these, other men of mark, politicians, statesmen, or soldiers—a company sitting silently wrapped away from all else, whilst,

[1] Afterwards Lady Lilford, almost the most beautiful head, Signor told me, from which he ever painted. He made several studies and used one of these as a type when painting the Alfred in his Lincoln's Inn fresco.

in the painter's mind, musician and music were being transferred to another art.

Mrs. Prinsep kept open house on Sunday afternoons in summer, and in the evening was also prepared for a party to remain for dinner; when the garden emptied, and tea and the games of croquet or of bowls were at an end, the big crimson sofas and seats, that looked so picturesque under the shade of the trees, were carried in, and this impromptu dinner-party followed. The evenings were filled up, either by music or by much delightful conversation, of such sort as was once described to me, when speaking of some special occasion, by a listener who said, "They talked of things that belonged to no date; their subjects would have interested men of any age." It was from the garden of Little Holland House that Sir John Herschel first saw the great comet of 1857, and here the drawing of his grand head was made and completed, all but the eyes. The astronomer's form of face and features are there, but empty space in place of the eye that had seen so far into the secrets of the universe. At this point the artist's hand held off, perhaps waiting for a special reserve of power, and to him it seemed never to come.

Some thirty years later he expressed his deep regret that he had not painted the portraits of two men—Darwin and Herschel. "The man of science should be better than any other," he said, "dwelling as he must in a kingdom of infinite wonder—larger than that of the poet or artist whose work of necessity turns him so much within himself and makes him think of and about his own emotions, and whose thoughts are necessarily more occupied with his own time and generation."

About this time Signor used to go round occasionally to Campden Hill, where Sir James South the astronomer then lived. There he looked through the great telescope at Saturn and his belt, and said that it was a sight that dwarfed all others.

When dining at Little Holland House, Mr. Doyle, who seems to be yet ever affectionately spoken of as Dicky Doyle, first met the Poet Laureate, and afterwards described how he had waited with bated breath to catch and treasure up the first syllables that should fall from his lips, expecting at least that such words should flow as, " He clasped the crag with hoöked hands," but no; the poet spoke—he said, "Legs of mutton should be cut in wedges." A very frequent guest at all times, Dicky Doyle came without fail on all Christmas Days, put his old umbrella into the stand on arriving, while it was taken for granted that he found a new one in its place on leaving, and not a word was said upon the subject.

From any mention, even by name, of the *habitués* at Little Holland House, the name of Mrs. Cameron (Julia Margaret), the sister of Mrs. Prinsep, cannot be omitted. To all who knew her she remains a unique figure, baffling all description. She seemed in herself to epitomise all the qualities of a remarkable family, presenting them in a doubly distilled form. She doubled the generosity of the most generous of the sisters, and the impulsiveness of the most impulsive. If they were enthusiastic, she was so twice over; if they were persuasive, she was invincible. "I had always to quarrel with Mrs. Cameron, that we might keep friends," was Signor's description of the attitude he had to adopt. If she had little of the beauty of her sisters, she certainly had remarkably fine eyes, that flashed like her sayings, or grew soft and tender if she was moved, perhaps when reading aloud some fine poem with modulations of voice and change of countenance, to which no one could listen unmoved. Like her eyes, her wit flashed out also. Her adoration for the author of *Philip Van Artevelde*, and for Lady Taylor, is well known; and it seems to have been borne by them with patience; or, at times, with impatience scarcely disguised. Their mutual friends had also to bear with her enthusiasms when they went somewhat beyond bounds, and the Poet Laureate's love of chaff was so far roused one day by her praises of Sir Henry Taylor's beauty as to say in banter, "I don't see what you mean by his extraordinary beauty—why he has a smile like a fish." But she retorted instantly, "Only when the Spirit of the Lord moved on the face of the waters, Alfred."

At Freshwater she commanded, and it was

done. Mr. Cameron once regretted that too much space was given up to vegetables in their garden. Her orders went forth secretly to friends and to henchmen that this must be remedied; but on no account could the work be done when Mr. Cameron wished to walk in the garden, which was every day. In cartloads, therefore, turf was brought and laid down out of view, and as soon as Mr. Cameron had gone to bed, her army was marshalled and, by lantern light, the vegetable garden was swept away; so when Mr. Cameron looked out next morning a fine grass lawn spread out before his astonished eyes. She used to describe how her letters to her sons in Ceylon were written up to the last possible moment. She would go on mail days to the General Post Office in London, and write there, crying out from time to time, " How much longer? " to which an enthralled clerk would reply, " Ten minutes more "—" five "—and so on, until the last second of time to be allowed had come, when her letter was shut and flung to the officials now waiting to seal up the last sack. She used to say that in her photography a hundred negatives were destroyed before she achieved one good result; her object being to overcome realism by diminishing just in the least degree the precision of the focus. Thus when a real success was attained, she was able to give to her work a poetry and a mystery far removed from the work of the ordinary photographer, far even from that of the very best who have followed her. While other photographs, after long acquaintance, weary the eye, hers remain always an abiding pleasure. She had much correspondence with Signor on the subject of principles of composition, and quotations from his words were often written below her pictures : " Quite Divine—G. F. Watts," under the photograph called the " Dream "—the profile of " Madonna " Mary, from whom most of Mrs. Cameron's successes were taken. Of some new batch of prints he writes : " All the heads are divine, and the plates very nearly perfect ; the tone too is excellent. If you are going on photographing your grandchild, and he is well worth it, do have a little shirt made of some yellowish material. The blot of formless white spoils the whole picture. What would not do in painting will not do in photography, but otherwise I am delighted with the amount of gradation you have obtained."

The same letter continues—" I have not time to write much, for I am very hard at work, trying to get ready for Freshwater. Amongst other things I am designing a St. John, one of four figures to be executed in mosaic for St. Paul's ; so my mind is tuned to a grand major key, and I can well appreciate what is noblest in art, and your last photographs harmonise well with the effects I wish to produce. But you must not be satisfied ; there is more to be done, and whilst this is the case we must never think anything done. I know your difficulties, but the greatest things have been done under difficulties."

In another letter he thanks her for photographs of Tennyson; some he considered magnificent, others he criticises and adds: "Do justice to the noble and beautiful head, the finest you will ever have before your lens. I have at last seen the new poems, and think the 'Northern Farmer' beyond all praise. It conveys to my mind the birth, parentage, education, life, and death of a whole community of rustics; nothing can be better or more complete." And again to Mrs. Cameron, when refusing a commission for a portrait, he writes:—

"Nature did not intend me for a portrait-painter, and if I have painted portraits decently it is because I have tried so very hard, but it has ever cost me more labour to paint a portrait than to paint a subject-picture. I have given it up in sheer weariness; now come what may, my time must in future be devoted to the endeavour to carry out some of my large designs, and if I fail either to make a living or to do anything worthy of an artist (as I understand the term), I fail, but I submit to the drudgery of portrait-painting no longer. . . .

"If I could carry out my own feeling perfectly, my pictures would be solemn and monumental in character, noble and beautiful in form, and rich in colour; but the subtle varieties of sunlight I should never aim at producing. I can see in nature what Turner saw, and can appreciate the excellence of his imitation, but my natural tendency is to see nature with such eyes as Giorgione and Titian had; I see only with their eyes, but do not work with their brains or hands. Alas!"

The reference made in the letter to Mrs. Cameron, to the design for one of the spandrils under the dome of St. Paul's, recalls that in 1861 Signor had been in correspondence with Dean Milman on the subject, having had occasion to write to the Dean to urge the fitness of his friend Charles Newton for the post of Keeper of Greek Antiquities at the British Museum; a post Mr. Newton—then Consul at Rome—was anxious to have. The Dean replies that he had the fullest appreciation of Mr. Newton's character and attainments, and continues: "You must allow me to add that if anything had been necessary to convince me of Mr. Newton's special fitness for the important office, your high opinion would have gone far. With regard to St. Paul's, it gives me the highest satisfaction to find that you take an interest in its embellishment; I shall carefully put your letter by, that when we arrive, as I trust we may (our only difficulty being funds), at the great question of mosaic ornament or fresco painting, we may avail ourselves at least of your counsel, if not—as I understand your generous offer—of more active and valuable support."

GEORGE FREDERIC WATTS

The result was the design for the two evangelists, St. Matthew and St. John, which were eventually carried out in mosaic, and it was Dean Milman's wish that Signor should be entrusted with the whole scheme of decoration; nevertheless after the Dean's death the matter was dropped.

To this time belongs the portrait of John Lothrop Motley. I find his letter appointing a sitting in May 1861, and remember that once, when we were reading over old letters that had escaped destruction, we came on this note; and my husband told me, out of his varied experience, that of all his sitters Motley was by far the finest talker he had ever come across. Signor used to quote against himself an example of no memory for faces: that a few years after these sittings he had allowed himself to be reintroduced to Motley, as to a stranger; Motley exclaiming, "Well, that is rather too bad, considering you have painted me twice." The following year he was staying at Blickling during several weeks, painting the portrait of Lord Lothian; a portrait of which Mr. Meredith wrote, on seeing it many years afterwards, that he was struck "by the living intelligence in the eyes, a point rarely achieved. I remember it at this moment only in the Titian Schoolmaster; as it is called generally." Signor was deeply interested in the subject of this portrait, impressed as he was by the beauty of character, rare intelligence, and the rich promise of a young life never to be fulfilled; for he knew he was painting a doomed man. All that medical skill and all that absolute devotion could do, was to be of no avail; and the tragedy of it seemed heightened by its passing in this poetically beautiful home. Life truly in flower at its best and loveliest; and so it was that the sight of Death inexorable, and Love impotent, came before his eyes. Here he painted in two hours' time the head of Lord Shrewsbury, Lady Lothian's father. Lady Waterford had asked him to show her his way of handling oil-colour, or rather *one* of the ways of setting about to paint a portrait, for his usual method took far more time; he seldom finished a picture at what the French call the first blow. Certainly, considering the subtleties of form and colour, he never surpassed that feat, excepting perhaps in the portrait of Sir Leslie Stephen painted many years later. He was also at work for his own pleasure on a portrait group of the three sisters, Lady Lothian, Lady Gertrude,[1] and Lady Adelaide Talbot;[2] and he made a study from the head of their brother,[3] for a picture he named the " Standard-Bearer " : this was done in the hope that he should some day paint a life-size equestrian portrait of Lord Shrewsbury in armour, representing some ancestor, with his son Reginald as standard-bearer, walking beside the horse. The project never went

[1] Afterwards Countess of Pembroke.
[2] The Countess Brownlow.
[3] General the Honourable Sir Reginald Talbot.

beyond a small sketch, painted in water-colour, and now placed between the two portraits in the collection at Compton. This visit to Blickling, and later another to Ingestre, Lady Lothian's old home, remained, in spite of the cloud on the horizon, a very happy recollection.

The great interest he found in Lady Waterford's work, the rides through wood and glade with pleasant companionship, the beginning of a friendship accorded to him through life by the family, all combined to leave a charming impression on mind and memory. He described one evening when out walking with a party, they suddenly saw Lady Waterford coming to join them, moving along so grandly that both he and the friend at his side could only exclaim in a breath, "O Pallas Athene!"

In the following year, 1863, to consider the need of a separate building for the Royal Academy—at that time occupying a part of the National Gallery—and other measures for extending its usefulness, a Royal Commission was held, before which the President, Sir Charles Eastlake, and several members of the Academy, with a few outside of this body, were called to give evidence. Amongst these last were John Ruskin, Holman Hunt, and G. F. Watts. The general tenor of Signor's evidence reveals his ever-constant desire that the Academy should stand as a great national institution for the encouragement of great art, and for the elevation and cultivation of the national taste; and that it should be recognised as a body entirely devoid of the element of a personal and professional clique.

For this reason he proposed that there should be a certain proportion of non-professional men elected as Members of Council; and he did not think the want of practical technical knowledge in these lay members would be in the least degree an objection. He considered that the non-professional element might more fairly represent the opinion "out of doors" than could the general body of artists themselves. "The non-professional man would be without predilections,—not entirely—no one is—but without any special taste for one style of painting." In the schools he strongly advocated a reform in the system of teaching, especially in the antique school, the most important of all, as there the pupils lay the foundations of all art—the drawing of the human figure.

He suggested that a specially competent teacher should be always there, and that while the students drew from casts, demonstrations should also be given from time to time from the living model. "I would demonstrate the action of the limbs, and the use of the muscles, from the living model in combination with the antique. It is impossible to learn much about the human form by merely drawing the figure in a set position."

He would like to see sculpture, painting, and architecture connected together as one and the same; and that students should be encouraged to study the whole range of art as much as possible. "I look upon architecture as one of the most important branches of art. I lament the *three branches*; they were not considered as three formerly, but were combined in one and the same man."

The more they are combined the better it would be for art in general. Above all things he wanted to see the Royal Academy students, under the supervision of an accomplished artist, trained to make designs, or even to copy designs, such as Flaxman's, upon wall spaces and on a large scale; not only because he considered that the practice of mural painting was of paramount importance, but that also it might lead to a more general diffusion of art, giving the public a very much greater opportunity of seeing something beautiful, both in colour and line. "At present," he wrote to Lord Elcho, one of the Commissioners, a few days after giving his evidence, "it is a melancholy fact that hardly a single object amongst those that surround us has any pretension to real beauty, or could be put simply into a picture with noble effect; and, as I believe the love of beauty to be inherent in the human mind, it follows that there must be some unfortunate influence at work. To counteract this should be the object of a Fine Art Institution, and I feel assured that if really good things were scattered amongst the people, it would not be long before satisfactory results exhibited themselves."

GEORGE FREDERIC WATTS

Lord Elcho propounds the grave question, with mischief lurking in his look, no doubt, " Is the system a sound one in your opinion, of giving panels in a corridor to different artists, to be decorated according to their own notions ? " " I disapprove of it very much, the result of it must be inharmonious." And again in the same spirit he asked the question, "Whether, under arrangements more favourable to the selection of the best art for our public places, we should have had at the present moment the Duke of Wellington's statue on the arch at Hyde Park"; and Mr. Watts replies, " I think there would have been a chance that we should have had a better thing." It is clear that the Commissioner and his witness understood each other.

The Chairman, Lord Stanhope, asks, " Have any other points occurred to you in which you think alterations for the better might be made in the Royal Academy?" Mr. Watts replies, "It is very difficult to point out how the Academy might be improved, and I have not given much attention to the subject; but, considering the position the Academy holds, it has displayed very great apathy. I do not see its influence in our architecture, our fashions, or our taste in general, in any way whatever. The only National School which has grown up at all has grown up outside the Academy, and indeed in opposition to it, that is the Water Colour School; and the only definite reform movement (which the Pre-Raffaelite School may be called) was certainly not stimulated by the Royal Academy, and even met with opposition from it."

Chairman: "You ascribe the fact which you have mentioned to some defect in the Royal Academy?" "It seems to me that there must be some defect. If the members were extremely anxious to develop taste, or to encourage art, I think that some means could have been found. A merchant finds means if he wants to improve his commercial arrangements; whatever a man wishes to do he finds a way of doing it more or less satisfactorily. But I do not see that the Royal Academy has done anything whatever.

"I must beg to say, in making these remarks, that I have no kind of feeling against the Royal Academy. Many of the members whom I have the honour to be acquainted with I esteem very much indeed. They have always displayed to me great consideration, and indeed kindness, and as I was never a candidate for the honour of membership I cannot say that I have been overlooked; and I have not the smallest personal feeling of any kind against them."

In the supplementary letter to Lord Elcho, after giving evidence before the Royal Academy Commission, Signor wrote: "I insist upon mural painting for three reasons—first, because it is an exercise of art which demands the absolute knowledge only to be obtained by honest study, the value of which no one can doubt, whatever branch of art the student might choose to follow afterwards; secondly, because the practice would bring out that gravity and nobility deficient in the English school, but not in the English character, which being latent might therefore be brought out; and, thirdly, for the sake of action upon the public mind."

Of the benefit of studying the old masters he wrote: "The great Italian masters worked unquestionably upon some principle (for technique); no one can undervalue the practical importance of placing at the disposition of the student means of expressing his ideas much sooner than he could possibly find them out for himself."

During these years Signor, having some occasion to consult an oculist, was recommended to go to Mr. Bowman, whose reputation for skill and delicate manipulation he had been aware of for some years. They were kindred spirits; as those who may happen to remember Sir William Bowman will understand—"a nature finely touched to fine issues," and a great lover of art and literature. He had seen the painter's own portrait—painted, I believe, some years before, for Signor told me it had been "knocking about for some time in the studio, and at last Bowman much wished to have it," and the last portrait of the Poet Laureate as well. As was very much his habit, he had hesitated about price, fearing that he was asking too much, and Mr. Bowman replies:—

"*17th November* 1863.

"MY DEAR MR. WATTS—I really can on no account let you off, so I have the pleasure of enclosing a cheque for one hundred guineas ; and why should I take a tenth of you ? I am no parson !

"I am delighted to hear you propose soon to finish for me the head of the great poet. The sooner the better. The only thing I would have wished otherwise in the head of the great artist, is that in size and handling it does not (but perhaps my impression is wrong) match the other ; for I would fain have painter and painted, a pair of nobles answering one to the other on my walls. Shall you ever treat yourself 'with variations' ? If so, may I have the only *locus penitentiae* I can ever desiderate ? But believe me I fully appreciate the true humility and delicacy of mind which dictated your note of to-day.—Always truly yours,

"W. BOWMAN."

Preserved in the same envelope with this note is a letter from Ruskin of almost the same date—18th November 1863.

"DEAR WATTS—Indeed I love you much, and it was *not* ill-treatment of you. I was too ill to see any one, it would only have hurt you to see *me* : so tired and sad I was about many things. *Now* I have given up everything but friends—and dinners, so judge if I won't come and dine with you.* I shall like to see you all again so much. Only I am just home for a week just now. I'm going into the country on Monday,

G. F. Watts

*(a portrait bequeathed by Sir William Bowman Bart.
to the National Gallery of British Art)*

and I can't arrange for anything before that ; but I'll be back in no time and at home all the winter. I mean to try and see you in the forenoon before Monday, but mayn't be able, but I think I shall.—Always affectionately yours,

"J. RUSKIN.

" *P.S.**—Not that I would dine with many people, because friends and dinner are too good to have at once : I like to eat like a bear, and hug afterwards, but to growl over my bones."

During these years Mr. Ruskin seems to have been often and much at Little Holland House, and the following little note, evidently written from Denmark Hill, shows what he had lately been looking at in the studio :—

"14*th* May 1864.

" DEAR WATTS—I find all my apple-blossoms (nearly) on the ground this morning in fading snow, so I won't let you come to me for a fortnight yet, when I shall have got some flowers out and some strawberries ripe, I hope, and some of Jones's sketches framed ; but I shall beg of you to come then, very earnestly.

" That haystack and Colleone[1] and the new Trionfo della Morte Madonna stay by me—but you know—you *must* learn to paint like Titian ! —Ever affectionately yours,   J. RUSKIN."

[1] The words haystack and Colleone refer to the small landscape called " All the air a solemn silence holds," an impression he received when riding home one evening ; both stacks and trees were close to Little Holland House. The other picture is known as " The Court of Death."

GEORGE FREDERIC WATTS

In the spring of 1864 Garibaldi came to England to receive an ovation, which appears to have exceeded in enthusiasm all such for many years before or since. The admiration of the crowd for their hero put his life, at one part of the progress from the station to Stafford House, into as much danger as it had ever been during his campaigns! Signor, as a true sympathiser with the emancipation of Italy, who admired him greatly, had arranged with the Duchess of Sutherland to attempt to make a portrait of him, but the sittings had to be from seven to eight in the morning, and even then there were deputations waiting below to pay him homage. The duchess came herself and read aloud to the patient sitter. There was a study made of the head, as well as a more finished picture; and of this portrait the Countess Martinengo Cesaresco wrote in 1903: "I sent one of Mr. Hollyer's photographs of your beautiful portrait of Garibaldi to his surviving son, General Ricciotti Garibaldi, whose acquaintance I made lately in Rome. I have just had a letter from his wife, in which she says, 'My husband received the portrait with the greatest pleasure; it is most wonderfully like!'

"I feel a temptation to send this little word to you, and I hope that you will pardon the liberty I take in doing so."

In spite of the constant intercourse Signor had for years enjoyed with friends, many of whom, sooner or later, have been given their

GEORGE FREDERIC WATTS

place in making the history of their time; in spite of the solicitous care given to him by all at Little Holland House, and the real affection in which he was held by the whole circle of the family, there is often a note of great sadness in his letters. A sense of loneliness seems to pervade his life. Perhaps this is the case even in the happiest surroundings, where the nature has been given intimations of some place afar, which it is ever seeking, partly aware that only there can it ever be truly at home. In more than one letter I find that he expresses regret that he had never married; as if he were asking himself whether it was this companionship that was missing from his life. To what is well known I wish to add nothing; all who have heard his name know also that a beautiful young girl who, with her yet undeveloped genius, was destined later to fascinate and delight thousands of her generation, came into his life, that they were married in February 1864, and were parted in June 1865, and, except for the accident of one chance meeting in the streets of Brighton, never met again, the marriage being dissolved in 1877.

But to return to what had just been said, of the something akin to loneliness that contributed to make him know a tinge of sadness, as if for some reason he was not quite at home in the ways of life, a feeling which is probably shared by all highly sensitive natures, and to be accounted for by their spiritual elevation. That this elevation was visible in him can best be explained by the effect his presence had upon others. After the last visit Mr. F. W. H. Myers paid to Signor, he wrote of him as " one who without sect or dogma shall answer to the welcoming Infinite with simplicity and calm." Or, in the simple words used by a French lady who, forty years later, looking back to her early teens, said, " Mr. Watts was the first person to make me want to be good." It was not an aloofness, which would have put a distance between him and you—this was never so; it seemed as natural to be aware of that elevation as to be aware of the air breathed on a mountain top—you were beside him, but on a plane that you knew was different. Not long ago I had the pleasure of talking to a lady at Brighton who had known him well in these early 'sixties. She spoke with enthusiasm and affection of many of his friends, and describing one brilliant personality after another, ended by saying, " But Mr. Watts was different—he had something apart."

In 1865 the introduction of Mr. Charles Rickards to Signor, through the medium of Mr. J. E. Taylor and his namesake, though not related, Mr. Tom Taylor (author and critic), was the means of bringing a very sincere admirer and constant purchaser of pictures to the studio at Little Holland House. Mr. Rickards wished to have a portrait painted by him, and from the time of their first acquaintance kept all the letters and notes that passed between them for more than twenty years. They are docketed by him as "Letters written to me by my friend, preserved by me from motives of warm regard, as well as for the future biographical or other public service.—C. H. Rickards." These letters were kindly given to me in 1904 by his cousin, Miss Chesworth. The first of the bundle is from Tom Taylor to his namesake :—

"17th June 1865.

"Dear Taylor—I have written urgently to Watts *re* Rickards, pointing out to him how important it is that the great North should be impregnated with great Art of a different character from much of that which enriches your picture dealers, and fills the galleries they have the catering for.—Always yours,
"Tom Taylor."

The first sitting for this portrait was in September 1865, the artist having told Mr. Tom Taylor that it could not be painted out of hand, as he had much work about in his studio, to complete which he was giving all the time possible. The portrait was therefore not finished until the end of September in the year following, and when appointing the last sitting Signor writes : "I am glad to find that the subject of art is become one of interest to you, and I hope, from what you say, to some of your friends. I am sure that you now feel it is an interest that should not be left out of any man's life. However little I might care about being known myself, I am glad that the opinions I have arrived at by really earnest thinking should be known and tested. In the belief that art of noble aim is necessary to a great nation, I am sometimes tempted in my impatience to try if I cannot get subscriptions to carry out a project I have long had, to erect a statue to unknown worth—in the words of the author of *Felix Holt*, 'a monument to the faithful who are not famous.' I think this would be a worthy thing to do, and if I had not unfortunately neglected opportunities of making money, I would certainly do it at my own expense.

"I am at this time making a monumental statue, and feel confident I could execute a colossal bronze statue that should be a real monument. I would give up all other work to be enabled to carry out such an idea, and should be contented if guaranteed against loss ; contented to be able to meet the expenses of the undertaking. Please think a little about this plan."

When the portrait and another picture were about to be sent off to Mr. Rickards, he writes : "I will send the pictures in a day or two, and I must ask you to hang them on a dark wall ; an oil picture suffers so very much if hung upon a light ground. If your walls are light I would beg you, for the sake of your own pleasure in the pictures, to have your room re-papered. It may seem a rather bold request, but pictures are expensive luxuries, and a man ought to get all the satisfaction he can out of them, and, I may say, in justice to the artist. Any dark colour, red or green, and no matter how rich, would do, and if possible the picture should be hung with the light on the spectator's left, and not too near the window, because the spectator should stand between the pictures and the light."

The portrait of Mr. Rickards gave entire satisfaction, and to him Mr. Frederick Walker,[1] an intimate friend, writes of this: "It is no exaggeration to say that it is the best portrait I have ever seen of one intimately known to me. The features are drawn with photographic avoidance of flattery, and at the same time the noblest side of your character appears." In this letter he also says that he agrees with Signor that frescoes might be invaluable instruments of education. It had occurred to him some years ago, on seeing the fresco at Lincoln's Inn, that with the aid of the sixth book of the *Æneid*, Roman history could be well condensed into a single picture. "There in the Elysian fields Anchises points out to Æneas the unborn souls of all the men who in after times were to make Rome great, the long list ending with Pompey, Cæsar Augustus, the young Marcellus. Perhaps the subject is not susceptible of picturesque treatment, but I should like to see the experiment tried." To this Signor replies: "You may be sure that I am most gratified to find your friends approve. Some success such patience as yours insured; but, anxious as I

---

[1] In later years headmaster of St. Paul's School.

am, I never feel sure of succeeding under any circumstances, as portraiture is certainly not my line, and I find it very difficult, hence it is that I undertake a portrait with very great reluctance, but my pleasure in giving satisfaction is of course in proportion. I am much interested by Mr. Walker's letter and certainly sympathise with his idea. What he proposes is exactly the right kind of thing for educational purposes, and exactly the right treatment of the subject. Ten years ago I would have offered to paint a mural picture of the kind, provided the materials were found. It is not in my power to do so now, but I would gladly make some sacrifice in order to carry out so admirable a scheme. Your Manchester School of Art ought to be able to supply students competent to carry out designs under the direction of an experienced artist. Surely something might be done in such a place as Manchester."

In the next letter, some six months later, he writes: "Flattered as I must be by your wish to buy some of my pictures, I feel great difficulty about taking advantage of your newly awakened taste. It is possible you may hereafter regret spending money upon works which may never be generally cared for; at the same time, as I naturally think my direction a right one, or I should not follow it, and—as I am desirous of giving an impulse to taste for art of a graver and nobler character than that which is characteristic of the English school, you shall have such pictures of mine as you may take a fancy to, upon the understanding that I take them back at the same price if you should change your opinion of them, or grow tired of them." Later in the same letter he writes: "I shall keep you to your offer to purchase a picture from some young artist, and will take care that you shall run no risk. Thank you for the promise. As to the criticisms—even the best art critics are very unsafe guides, talking more glibly than wisely, upon the subject; even when they form—speaking generally—a right estimate of the excellencies of the picture, mostly praising it for qualities it does not possess, and disapproving of qualities which really are merits, so that real artists who began by resenting their patronage as much as their blame, soon become indifferent to both."

Again, three months later, he writes to Mr. Rickards: "I have always told you that I feel the greatest unwillingness to take advantage of your wish to buy so many pictures, lest I should be injuring you and defrauding others. However, we have discussed that matter, and I won't say more about it"—a promise he felt himself unable to keep; and over and over again Mr. Rickards is warned that he may be defrauding him, or that those who come after him may feel that his investments in these pictures were ill-judged; and often he had to apologise for returning Mr. Rickards's cheque, if sent before the picture was completed, or if in payment of one he could not make up his mind to sell. "The Court of Death" was designed and well advanced. "Time, Death, and Judgment" was also designed. The small version of "Sir Galahad" had been completed before 1862. The study for the head of the knight was made from Arthur Prinsep as early as 1855 or 56. "The Court of Death" was originally designed for a Mortuary Chapel. Signor had been told of a project to open a cemetery for London paupers, in which a chapel was to be built where the coffins would be collected, to ensure that one burial service would be sufficient for several paupers. This cold calculation to save trouble had touched Signor to the quick, and he immediately set to work to think out such a design as he believed might dignify the building. The scheme for this cemetery was, I believe, given up, certainly in its original bareness. Of this design and of his "Time, Death, and Judgment" he writes to Mr. Rickards: "Allegory is much out of favour now and by most people condemned, forgetting that spiritual and even most intellectual ideas can only be expressed by similes, and that words themselves are but symbols. The design 'Time and Death' is one of several suggestive compositions that I hope to leave behind me in support of my claim to be considered a real artist, and it is only by these that I wish to be known. I am very glad that you find the ring of poetry in it."

CHAPTER VIII

THOUGHT and imagination are the attributes of man alone. Surely the development of the conception of beauty indicates an assimilation to the most divine—that which is most beyond our mere material existence.

G. F. WATTS.

CHAPTER VIII

ON Thursday, January 31, 1867, Edward Armitage and George Frederic Watts were elected Associates of the Royal Academy, William Holman Hunt standing next in the order of votes.

These elections were made without the candidates putting down their names. When the news was brought to him by his friend Leighton, no one was more surprised by the result of the election than Signor himself. He had given his opinion at the Royal Academy Commission that the regulation by which each candidate for admission into that body was required to write his name down every year until elected was "vexatious and unnecessary."

"I know," he had said, "within the range of my own personal acquaintance, that it has been felt to be very disagreeable to many men." He thought that every man should be eligible who had been an exhibitor for any length of time. After Sir Charles Eastlake's death, Sir Francis Grant being President he worked to get this rule altered, and he afterwards told

Signor it was chiefly on his account. Signor's first impulse was to refuse the honour, on the ground that the state of his health precluded any possibility of his being useful in the Academy. He explained that the uncertainty of his condition made ordinary social life for him impossible, and kept him almost entirely in the seclusion of his studio. However, his friends Leighton and Armitage, and several members of the Academy, all pointed out to him the opportunities he would have for usefulness. Mr. Armitage wrote: "You would be able to give a vote at the election, and any opinion you expressed would, I am sure, have great weight with the junior members, and indirectly on the state of public feeling about art." He also says: "I was in hopes that in the Academy we might have united to give a new direction to the school." On February 7 Mr. Armitage again writes: "No one can rejoice more than I do that you have withdrawn your resignation; your note gave me very great pleasure." No doubt the opinion of his friend Leighton, who had been elected as Associate in 1864, had weight with him. In such matters it would; but he was also sensible that there was liberality in the action of the members of the Academy, as he had not conformed to rules, and was personally unknown to by far the larger number of the members, who might very well consider that he was critical of the Institution, if not hostile to it. His election as Academician followed in December of the same year, which, he thought, was generous; though some of his friends considered it to be "but tardy justice," as his work had been before the public for twenty-three years, and over and over again men, much his junior, had in the meantime been elected. However that may have been, there was no feeling of soreness on his part; and in 1869 he was busy, with his friend Frederic Leighton, at work as one of the Hanging Committee for the summer Exhibition. With them Sir Francis Grant had some difference of opinion on the subject of two pictures, which they refused to place on "the line," although the President had received—with one of them at least—a special request from high places to have it well hung. He writes afterwards: "You and Leighton acted with Roman virtue according to your judgment. . . . However, although we have differed, it has always been done in good humour; and I can assure you as friends I value you both greatly, and I am only happy to have seen so much of you, and to remember so much that has been so pleasant and agreeable. With the only trifling exception of the two pictures, I think I never remember to have seen the exhibition so well hung, and I never before have seen such general satisfaction. I am so sorry to hear you are poorly—you want another room to hang!"

The two friends had been given a very free hand in the matter of arrangement, but when they chose to hang their own pictures above "the line," their colleagues objected, and they were obliged to give way.

Many of Signor's well-known designs belong to these years, though few indeed can be said to belong to one year only. A design laid in in the 'fifties might be completed ten, twenty, and even thirty years later. He could not be persuaded to see his own work from the point of view of the expert of the future, who would require to place such-and-such work in an early or late period of the artist's life.

Mr. Thoby Prinsep, who was not æsthetic, grew impatient at times, and was once heard to exclaim, "I never saw such a fellow as you are, Signor! Why don't you finish one picture before you begin another?" and from the doorway came the parting shot from Signor as he went back to work, "My dear friend, you don't paint a picture as you would make a pair of boots!"

If, while it was still unfinished, he could improve a picture in any way, he would work upon it for any number of years. He very rarely retouched a completed work, one which, after some four or five years—the time he usually allowed for the colour to harden—he had had varnished. The only exception to this that I know of is the "Fata Morgana," now in the Municipal Gallery at Leicester. This picture, painted at Careggi, had been laid in with the simplicity of fresco. In 1889 he had all the mastic varnish removed from the picture, and in a very few days changed it from one thinly painted, laid in in broad simple masses, into a picture extremely rich in texture and brilliant in colour. I remember Sir Frederic Leighton chaffing him about the "*tocchi resoluti*," and for once approving of this union of two periods of manner. His counsel was usually against delay in completing pictures, the two friends differing very distinctly. Signor often begged Leighton not to attempt to finish for exhibition in May pictures he had begun in the autumn. They talked things over, but each went his own way; it could not have been otherwise.

I must here venture to correct an error that has appeared more than once in published accounts of Mr. Watts's work with reference to a portrait of Lady Somers, begun in 1860. It is a mistake to say that he worked all over this in 1889. The right arm, sleeve, and lower part of the picture had originally been sketched in monochrome, and so left. Naturally, the colour painted over these parts in 1889 is distinguishable from that which was painted thirty-eight years before; but he put no touch upon the panel where the work was already complete, save only on one small spot upon the lower lip, where there was some slight damage to the colour.

The designs he had now in hand were the "Court of Death," "Time, Death, and Judgment," "The Creation," "The Denunciation," "The Genius of Greek Poetry," "The Island of

Cos," "Ariadne in Naxos," "Daphne," "Thetis," and "The Mid-day Rest." Besides these, he was at work upon a full-length portrait of Lady Bath, now at Longleat. It was carried on during more years than he could remember, that subtle quality of resemblance eluding him. He asked Lady Bath once, during the last sittings, if she could remember when the portrait was begun, and she answered, "I am not quite sure of the exact date, but I know it was soon after my marriage, and now I have seven children."

It was at this time that Mr. Gladstone wrote [1] to express a wish to possess the picture described in the catalogue of the Royal Academy Exhibition of 1868 as "The Wife of Pygmalion, a translation from the Greek," and in reply Mr. Watts writes thus :—

"*May 3rd*, 1868.
"LITTLE HOLLAND HOUSE.

"DEAR MR. GLADSTONE—I am really rather shocked by your great admiration of the 'Wife of Pygmalion,' for it makes me feel like a humbug. I cannot think you could find her so deserving on longer acquaintance. In proportion as I value I am encouraged by sympathy with the direction of my efforts, having, I believe, a right to feel that they are worthy of some respect. I am really pained by applause which

---

[1] This letter is not preserved, but of the picture Mr. Bernard Bosanquet wrote to me in 1886 : "Ever since I saw the 'Galatea,' I have hung on Mr. Watts's works as the one realisation of what modern art might do. He has kept alive the conception of great art almost single-handed."

is more than my due ; if you will come out here some day I will cure you of your love and console you from your disappointment (the picture is claimed), by showing you the fragment from which it was painted, wherein you will see all that you admire in the picture, with infinite beauties altogether missed.

"I much desire your good opinion of my bust (The Clytie), and must explain that my aim in this my first essay has been to get flexibility, impression of colour, and largeness of character, rather than purity and gravity—qualities I own to be extremely necessary to sculpture, but which, being made, as it seems to me, exclusively the objects of the modern sculptor, have deadened his senses to some other qualities making part—often glories—of ancient Art, and this has resulted in bare and cold work. When you have time I should like to talk this matter over with you, for I have it much at heart, and I am full of anxiety to do something for the national honour. Mr. Jones and myself hope to avail ourselves of your invitation next Thursday.

"You may believe that I should be proud to know my 'Greek' head hung up in your house, but I am sure a cast of the antique bust will more than console you.—Yours very sincerely,
"G. F. WATTS."

Some years before, Sir Charles Newton and Signor had visited Oxford, to look over the Arundel Marbles. These marbles, though presented in 1624, had been left, in great part, neglected in a cellar. The object of their visit was to look over the fragments, and to pick out those which were of real worth for exhibition in the Ashmolean Museum. Signor was the discoverer here of a beautiful head severed at the neck, and unhappily without the nose. The missing parts were searched for, and they were successful in finding the bust and shoulders. It is now one of the gems of the collection. Signor ranked this bust with the best art of Greece in the time of Pheidias, but he believed that it was a portrait, because certain characteristics of the Greek ideal were lacking. For instance, the eyes were slightly prominent, which alone denoted that it was a likeness. Casts were made from the bust, and one of these always stood in his studio. The reverence in which this was held by him was so great that it inspired him to paint the transition of Galatea from marble to life. To compare this picture with the Greek bust is instructive, the attempt is so often made to discover plagiarisms committed by our poets, a form of criticism from which Shakespeare does not escape. Had the picture been in any way a copy of the bust, it could not have been ranked, as it was by Mr. Gladstone and others, as amongst the painter's most imaginative works. All art is transmitted by a natural process of fertilisation. Almost unconsciously this process had stirred his imagination. From his letter to Mr. Gladstone, it is clear that Signor looked upon his picture as a sort of portrait of the bust. But how far it is removed from this, comparison of the two will show. The distinction between a copy and the work inspired by the great work of another artist's imagination is evident. The imitator of any school, or of any artist's productions, must in his own production fall so short of the original that he can never hope to stir the enthusiasm of the spectator.

To a young student I have heard Signor say: "Go and look at the old masters, not to copy them but to admire them; look at Nature and be yourself. Learn the principles of art, but never mind about the rules; they may be broken, and are by every great painter; the principles are fundamental."

Great Art and great Nature fertilise the minds of those gifted to receive; for as Walt Whitman says, "The great masters hear the inaudible words of the earth."

One full-length portrait was painted during these years, and is now the best known of the portraits because it has been so generously lent to various exhibitions in London. It is one that probably to his mind came nearer than any other towards that attainment to style always kept in view by him—the portrait of Mrs. Percy Wyndham. He proposed to begin this picture in the summer of 1866, but it was not begun till the spring of 1867, and was on the easel until the spring of 1870, when he hoped that he might complete it for exhibition at the Academy; but he writes later to say he is so unwell that he has given up all idea of sending it. Though it was finished shortly after this date, it was not exhibited until the first exhibition at the Grosvenor Gallery in 1877. The painting of this portrait brought a new joy into his life, as he writes many years afterwards when he speaks of his regret at ever having finished it, because he saw Mrs. Wyndham less often. " But not the less you will believe that your friendship is very precious to me." In another letter of an earlier date he tells her that, through the letter he had just received from her, he had been entering keenly into her enjoyment of great art and great nature; and he says further: " What depresses me in general is not so much that I cannot give utterance to 'the thoughts that fill my heart to bursting'" (her own words), " though it is painful enough, but that people walk through all this glory, and only coldly recognise that something is round about them, interesting perhaps when they have time to think upon the matter, after business and the claims of society. With me it is like a religion, in fact, I believe it to be part of the same thing; the sense of the beautiful in the highest manifestations is religious. I am really moved—much more than pleased—that you should have been prompted to write me a long letter, for I take it as a proof that my own efforts have not altogether failed in helping you to take in what you have seen. . . . That you are reminded of me is precious to me, as a sign that in direction and intention my aspirations are in harmony with what you so truly appreciate. Alas, that aspiration and achievement should be so far apart."

During the last five or six years, he had been working much with clay. His "Clytie," a bust, had been completed; but the first large piece of sculpture was for a memorial—a life-sized figure —commissioned by his friend Mr. Reginald Cholmondeley, to commemorate his elder brother Thomas, whose career of usefulness and high endeavour had been too early closed by death, tragically soon after his marriage in 1864. This memorial, now in Condover Church, was placed there a few years afterwards.[1] In 1869 he undertook to make a recumbent figure of the Bishop of Lichfield, Doctor Lonsdale. At first his sculpture studio was but a small greenhouse put to this use, and there the "Clytie" was modelled; but for larger work he shared part of a studio in Gold-Hawk Road, where the sculptor Mr. Nelson was at work. The commission for the Bishop's monument was not accepted without

[1] The question whether this memorial was by Signor or the work of Mr. Reginald Cholmondeley having been publicly raised, a friend, Mrs. Baldwin Childe, wrote to the former to confirm her (correct) statement, and received the following reply : " The statue of Thomas Cholmondeley Owen is wholly mine.—G. F. Watts, December 20th, 1898."

A confusion had been made between this work and a memorial in the same chapel at Condover Church to Mrs. Reginald Cholmondeley, that her husband had designed and carried out with the aid of advice from Signor.

some hesitation, and Sir George Gilbert Scott, who was to design the base and canopy, seems to have misunderstood this, and wrote to Mr. Watts saying that, in the event of his not undertaking the work, it would be offered to Mr. Armstead. Mr. Watts had replied in his usual generous way anxious to leave the commission to fall to the lot of another; and Sir Gilbert Scott writes to thank him for the manner in which he had received his letter. "You have, however, carried your generosity far beyond what I had intended, which had been suggested solely by your expressions of doubt as to your acceptance of the commission. It was only in case these doubts should be confirmed that I ventured to offer the suggestion I made. I feel that for you to decline the work when these doubts have been removed will be to deprive it of the benefit of the highest talent that could be devoted to it, and of which I cannot over-state my appreciation. I beg, therefore, that you will reconsider what the impulse of generosity has dictated."

The letters in which this spirit of generosity is referred to are many; sometimes on his returning a cheque for a portrait that has been criticised, sometimes when it was a question of hanging a work of his less well than his colleagues at the Royal Academy knew to be his due. On his exhibiting for the first time as an Associate there was a question of this sort; and Mr. George Richmond wrote: "I must, though very tired, thank you for your kind and obliging message.

GEORGE FREDERIC WATTS

My colleagues felt that I was treading on very delicate ground when I sent a message to you. Your generous answer has convinced them that I have not mistaken my man, and we are all grateful to you." Very often this spirit appears when he is anxious to obtain the commission for a younger man, and he has stepped aside in his favour. His treatment of the Bishop's lawn sleeves and robe was, he believed, at that time unique. It brings to mind his careful observation of Pheidian work, shown in the letter already quoted, on the frescoes of Giotto at Padua, and their likeness to the work of Pheidias. It will be remembered that of the Greek sculptor he said, "By many folds he took away the importance of the mass, leaving the head and limbs free and uninterfered with, simple, massive, and important." He never saw the memorial when placed in Lichfield Cathedral, but Sir Gilbert Scott told him with honourable candour that to his regret the canopy had destroyed the figure. Of this effigy Signor writes to Mr. Rickards:—

"I am glad you like the Bishop, but imagine you did not think the likeness good; a probable thing, for the materials I had to work from were very unsatisfactory, until I got two photographs from Miss Lonsdale; but then the alabaster was already so much advanced that alteration was not possible. Such an effigy is a very different thing from a portrait for a drawing-room, and the kind of likeness required should be in accordance rather with an abstract idea than of a realistic character;

but I would have made a great difference in it, if the photographs had come to hand earlier."

In colder weather he was prevented from working with clay, on account of the damp and chill, its effect upon his health being very bad. This material he afterwards ceased to use altogether, and replaced it by the Italian *gesso grosso*. But though prevented from going to work in the damp studio, he tells Mr. Rickards that his mind was much occupied with the subject of sculpture, and in the following summer he writes : " I have been sculpturing a good deal lately, and the more I do in that way, the more confidence I feel in my power as a sculptor." Mr. Rickards, though not a very rich man, was now buying from him paintings of mythical and symbolic subjects, at a time when very few indeed cared to possess these, and his generous appreciation was met in the same spirit. Always anxious that he should not defraud his friend, he writes : " I am relieved to find that the last importation was not a disappointment to you or your friends. You know I am always afraid of trafficking upon your predilections for my works, dreading lest I may injure you in your pocket or your taste. I am always anxious to hear that you are satisfied and that your friends approve. For this last reason I am really gratified to find Mr. Maddox Brown expressing a favourable opinion ; for in addition to being an artist of real genius, his sentiment for art is in many respects so different from my own that it was hardly to be expected that he should find much to care for in my work. You have twice expressed a wish that the portrait that you have of me should be exhibited; this I should be most unwilling to have carried out, and hope you do not greatly set your heart upon it, for it would be really disagreeable to me; not that I see any reason against an artist painting himself, but the contrary. The most interesting gallery I know is the collection of artists' portraits, painted by their own hands, and I paint myself constantly; that is to say, whenever I want to make an experiment in method or colour, and am not in a humour to make a design. So there are other portraits of me, and if I live there may be many more, but I should not like to display them to the public. I should feel a sort of absurdity attaching to such a proceeding."

With an organisation peculiarly sensitive to pain, whether physical or mental, it will be easily understood that the appreciation of a few friends, whose opinion he could respect, helped him to become inured to the indifference of a public led by criticisms either ignorant or hostile. Mr. Rickards not only gave this sympathy, but gave it in a material shape, often possessing himself of pictures which had been painted many years before; and thus he had found one of the greater satisfactions in life, one which he rejoiced in sharing with a group of friends artistic or literary, who were capable of entering into his pleasure. He liked to ask his friends to come to luncheon and afterwards to take them round his rooms, enjoying each picture in turn, or making the acquaintance of some new acquisition. He was led by Signor's influence to admire the works of other and younger men, and an occasional commission, where it was very welcome, was given through him. Of one of the first of these he writes to Mr. Rickards: " As to your generous proposal respecting the money that was to buy a picture by some young artist, I can only say that your feeling does you infinite honour, and makes me proud to reckon amongst my friends Charles Rickards; but whichever way you desire generously to apply the money, you may be sure that I should be the last person to deprive you of your honest credit. I should like you to have this credit; I will surely find an opportunity of gratifying your good feeling." Monsieur Legros was then but little known in England, and a commission for a picture to be painted for Mr. Rickards was acceptable to him. Of this Signor writes: " I shall be very anxious to know how Legros's picture is liked. I do not expect that it will be much approved of at first, but I think you will find that its grave simplicity will make its effect in time." In the next letter he writes: " I am delighted to find that Legros's work is appreciated. I own it is rather more than I expected, fearing that the simplicity of the workmanship would be regarded as want of finish. I am sure it is a picture that will give you more and more pleasure, as you become used to it; there is in it all the poetry your friends have fancied, but it is the unconscious poetry of the bird's song, and not an elaborated effort, therefore so much more delightful, being perfectly natural—a most rare quality."

Mr. Rickards's high services as a citizen of Manchester having been acknowledged publicly, Signor writes to him : " I wish all testimonials were as well deserved. I don't see why, for fear of seeming to be a flatterer, I should not add my testimonial, and say that I believe that you belong to the class that has made England great, and would make any nation great, earnest, sincere, and courageous, sympathising with all that is good in action and great in aspiration, free from meanness, and impatient only of wrong-doing. Perhaps it signifies little whether such are Whig, or Tory, or Radical ; the cause of humanity is sure to be helped. For myself I honour you and your like."

In spite of the opinion he expressed now in writing to a friend—" I am specially unfitted to paint a portrait "—his friends refused to be persuaded ; and when Mr. Henry Bruce—then Home Secretary—now better known as Lord Aberdare, was asked to give sittings for a presentation portrait and to choose the painter, he wrote to beg Signor to undertake it, saying : " Of this let me assure you, with all earnestness and sincerity, that I desire you to undertake the task, not only because I hold you to be the first of living artists, but because it will always be a pleasure to me and mine to know that my portrait was the work of a valued friend." In his reply Signor again begs to assure Mr. Bruce of his own incapacity. "I am not a good portrait painter," he writes; "I know you will point to a certain amount of success, but if you knew what toil, anxiety, and positive pain that success represents, you would feel it is in no degree commensurate." He also explains further, " The best part of my life is gone, and I devote what remains to the endeavour to produce works that will be worthy contributions to the national honour. I am conscious that it will be only an endeavour, so the aspiration is not presumptuous." The appeal made by Mr. Bruce must have been hard to resist; but the painter was at the moment realising to the full the difficulty of achieving a successful portrait, for Carlyle was giving him sittings, and Signor was more than ever confirmed in the opinion that he was not intended by nature to succeed in portraiture, and Mr. Wells undertook the commission.

Carlyle was an impatient sitter, and though he tried to conceal the fact, Signor was conscious of this, and told me that it so acted upon his nerves that one of the most important portraits he had ever taken in hand was thus spoilt. "You have made me like a mad labourer," was Carlyle's well-known comment. In spite of this ruggedness of character, Signor's impression of Carlyle was one of goodness and nobility of disposition, and he thought that the emphasis, in Mrs. Carlyle's letters, upon his irritability, exaggerated what may have been a blemish in a childlike and generous nature. Three portraits of Carlyle were begun; two were completed and one left incomplete. The sittings had already begun in June 1867, perhaps earlier, and were still being continued in July of the following year, when Carlyle writes: "Unexpectedly I find I have to go to Scotland in about ten days, and continue there I know not how long. If you do want me again, therefore, let it be within that time, fairly within; I am anxious to neglect nothing for perfecting of our mutual enterprise, in which I see in you such excellent desire after excellence, and shall be ready within the prescribed limits and times, any time at a day's notice."

The two had many discussions, the artist in vain trying to open the eyes of the great prophet to the value of art outside the historical record in a portrait. Signor liked to tell his friends the opinion he gave him upon the works of Pheidias, and it has therefore become common property. Carlyle had been to see the Elgin Marbles, and stated that there was not one clever man amongst them, the jaw was not sufficiently prominent; and, he added, "depend upon it neither God nor man can get on without a jaw." He thought the long upper lip was a sign of intellect, though his opponent could quote Napoleon, and Byron, and Carlyle's hero Goethe, as being remarkable for the beauty of a very short one. He did not find in the frieze or any fragment from the Parthenon what he called "a clever man amongst them all, and I would away with them," he said, "away with them—into space." They also differed as to whether the brown eye or grey eye denoted the man of action, Carlyle maintaining that the brown eye belonged of necessity to the active temperament and the grey eye to the contemplative. Signor, denying this, could quote Guizot, who had seen Napoleon I. in Switzerland, and had told him he could never forget the steel-coldness of his eye. Carlyle sends a copy of an extract at the end of which he writes : " Mahomet's eyes were large, black, and full of fire (*Biographie Universelle*, tome 26, p. 206, by Silvester de Lacy). For its excellence and clearness, from which *you* might paint, I have had the whole description copied for you, and send it revised with my compliments.—T. Carlyle, Chelsea, June 18th, 1867."

In accordance with the regret he had expressed to the Commissioners then considering the state of the Royal Academy, that architecture, sculpture, and painting had ceased to be looked upon as one, and that artists were therefore in the habit of keeping exclusively to one branch, he was devoting himself more than ever to the study of sculpture, the adaptation of painting to architecture being denied to him. About 1867, for the larger work he had in hand, he felt the necessity of a sculptor's studio ; and, on obtaining permission from Lady

GEORGE FREDERIC WATTS

Holland to build this, he found with some alarm that there was no written promise to Mr. Prinsep that his lease — expiring in December 1871—would be extended. Signor therefore begged Lady Holland to allow him to enter into an agreement for an extension of ten years at any rental she might like to ask, the lease to be in his name; but she was then quite sure that she would never wish to make changes during her life, and seemed rather to smile at the idea that legal arrangements were necessary between them. The sculpture studio was therefore built, and there the Condover memorial was modelled. Four years later (1871) he was at work upon a memorial to Lord Lothian, for Blickling Church; and in correspondence with the Marquis of Westminster about a great equestrian statue of Hugh Lupus. While thinking of this group, he had at the same time sketched out in his mind the work he was anxious to make as great as might be, the embodiment of physical energy. He was therefore overwhelmed when he heard that Lady Holland was being advised, for the good of the estate, to sell off that part of Little Holland House garden on which his sculpture studio stood. To him it appeared to be the destruction of all privacy, all beauty, and even more: it seemed as if his hope of realising his desire to do one great work was to be taken from him. Being of nervous temperament, the change appeared to be a calamity, for he now realised that they had no guarantee that Little Holland House would continue to be leased to Mr. Prinsep after six months' time. So far they had felt secure, as Lord Holland had always given them to understand that he could never be tempted to destroy Little Holland House, the place being dear to him from old association; and Lady Holland, after his death, had confirmed this view herself, both to the Prinseps and to Signor. There was some friction, Signor writing his views very plainly, and believing that no money could compensate for the loss to the property of this pleasant old house with its fields and farm, so unique in its situation now that Kensington had become a part of London. To other arguments he adds : "You know that from the very outset of my career my one desire has been to prove myself a true artist, studying and labouring hard, in spite of want of health or means or encouragement, with the direct object of contributing my little—but my best—towards the enrichment not only of the nation but of humanity in general—aspirations perhaps in me ridiculous, certainly not ignoble. All my way through, clinging to this idea, I have abstained from throwing myself into popular art, resigning money-making (to the increase of my difficulties in the present juncture), but have steadily worked on, generally against discouragement, endeavouring by severe labour to acquire knowledge and experience, making large designs both in painting and sculpture with this great end in view." The outcome of this correspondence was nothing very definite; Lady Holland felt sure that she would not wish to make any change, yet at the same time she does not seem to have given any distinct promise, with the result that, at the end of the lease in 1871, the Prinseps became merely tenants by the year. Meanwhile Signor had bought some acres in the Isle of Wight, adjoining the Farringford property; for on learning that Lady Holland had received an offer for the site of Little Holland House, amounting to some forty thousand pounds, he told her that he withdrew any kind of suggestion that might "interfere with her prudential arrangements"; and he writes that "with any reference to the future, Little Holland House had," for him, "practically ceased to exist." He ends his letter, of which a copy exists, by telling her that he is now going to devote his time to painting portraits, with the object of making money for the purpose of building new studios. "Trouble and expense are before me," he writes, "but the only real misery to me arises from loss of time; and I must hope to live long enough to make that up. I have not spoken at all to the Prinseps about this, and shall not do so: the question of Little Holland House is now entirely between you and them, and I sincerely hope that with the removal of all difficulty between us, there may be a removal of all vexation. It would grieve me very much to feel any coolness between so old a friend and myself." The letter was addressed to St. Anne's Hill, bearing the date of December 3, 1871.

Lady Holland, as I have already said, granted a further extension by the year, and for three more years the Prinseps were her tenants.

It was in 1870 that the then Marquis of Westminster first asked Signor to consider the possibility of undertaking a big equestrian group to represent in sculpture what he called his mythical ancestor, Hugh Lupus (*Le Gros Veneur*), to be placed in one of the courts at Eaton Hall. Lord Westminster had at one time spoken to Sir Edward Landseer on the subject, but on referring again to this matter, Landseer had definitely replied that he was already too deeply engaged to venture on a fresh commission. This left the ground clear, and the offer was exceedingly agreeable to Signor, who writes: "What I should wish would be to have the materials and necessary aid provided and paid for by an agent of yours, and would gladly do my part for nothing, and think myself overpaid by the chance of distinguishing myself." Writing to Mr. Rickards, November 22, 1870, he says: "I don't know where you saw an account of the design for the equestrian statue; it had very little existence except in the poetical imagination of the writer. All that is, is the merest sketch on a very small scale, nothing to photograph. I hope it will start into form with the coming spring." The work was begun in this way at old Little Holland House, and carried on during 1873-74, though much disturbed by the prospect of change, and by the necessity for undertaking many portraits, that he might carry out his desire to provide a home at Freshwater, where he hoped his friend Mr. Prinsep[1] might yet enjoy many years of life and repose. For Signor himself, these early years of the 'seventies were full of vexation. There was the certainty that the home to which he had become attached was so soon to be destroyed—an uprooting peculiarly painful to his nature; and the new venture required money, which could only be made with anything like certainty by painting portraits. Of this he writes to Mr. Rickards: " No one can imagine the intense weariness of my existence as a portrait painter." It was really more than weariness; he was often prostrated by nervousness before the arrival of some new sitter; and, as he once said to me, " No one knows what it costs me, and yet when I take people's cheques, I feel as if I were cheating them." He had not quite completed the monument of the Bishop of Lichfield, nor was the statue of Lord Holland's father,[2] made more or less in conjunction with Mr. Boehm,

[1] Mr. Prinsep had suffered from various causes a considerable loss of fortune, the first of these causes being a contested election for a seat in Parliament, which threw unexpected expense upon him.
[2] In the park at Holland House; behind the fountain in High Street, which was the work of Sir Edgar Boehm.

yet out of hand; and he writes in June 1870 to say he was "too much overworked by the necessity of finishing sculpture I have on hand before the clay falls to pieces. I always get to work soon after 5 A.M. and work all day, so you may suppose I am rather done up, which is the reason I have not answered your letter." The Hugh Lupus he intended to be simply decorative with some suggestion of a time when violence and force were characteristic.

The Duke took great interest in the progress of the work, and wrote many letters referring Mr. Watts to the pattern of spurs, or of the actual sword supposed to belong to *Le Gros Veneur* preserved at the British Museum, and he sent to Normandy for a perfect specimen of a horse—the Normandy *Percheron*. It was brought over to Cliveden to be at Signor's service when he required it, and was photographed in the garden at Little Holland House. This statue was taken to the foundry at Thames Ditton in 1883. It took nine months to cast and was delivered at Eaton Hall in September 1884. The original work of the artist (in *gesso grosso*) was presented to the collection of casts at the Crystal Palace by the Duke of Westminster.

While working out the small sketch the thought occurred to him that on the same scale he would some day allow himself to design a group, untrammelled by costume or period; and almost simultaneously he made sketches for the "Physical Energy," which was eventually to be worked at during the fine weather, as the work was done out of doors. Dauntless as always in the tasks he set himself, he now proposed to undertake his diploma picture, and on December 31, 1870, he says: "I am now about to paint for the Royal Academy a picture containing six or seven life-sized figures"; and this picture was completed and exhibited in the May following. As he never devoted himself exclusively to any one picture, believing that it was better for hand and eye to be kept alert and awake by turning from one train of thought and its artistic expression to quite another, and yet another successively, it was an unusual feat for him to have carried out so large a design in such a very short time. The picture, hanging as it does in the little-visited Diploma Gallery, is not well known. During the exhibition of 1872 the effect of the work was so far neutralised by the strong contrasts beside it that in consequence he asked permission of the Council to be allowed to work upon the picture after the exhibition had closed, and arriving there one day with his materials for work, the Royal Academy porter, who carried these for him, on entering the now empty gallery, stopped short in surprise and exclaimed, "Why, sir, it's a different picture"; and Signor found that there was nothing he wished to change. This picture awaits the judgment of time. The name in the catalogue was "My Punishment is greater than I can bear"—later known as the " Denunciation of

Cain"; it is one of the fragments of the "House of Life." In his mind a sort of epic grew up about this early record of a crime, the brother's hand against a brother. He believed it to be a subject for a great cantata, and now and again tried to give shape to it in words; but nothing he wrote seemed to him adequate, and these remain only in fragmentary notes. In speaking of it, he once outlined the general idea in this way:—

"If I were a poet and musician like Wagner, I could make a fine cantata or oratorio of the subject. The first act would be to describe the innocence of the two brothers in their boyhood, the first shadow of the stain in the character of Cain just indicated; then, as the story grew, to mark the widening difference between them— the angelic guilelessness of Abel and the darkening of Cain's heart through the sin of jealousy, the ever-increasing desire to make himself greater than Abel ending in the madness of his wrath and the murder of Abel. The denouncing spirits, as I have painted them, represent the voices of conscience reproaching him with the many sins that culminated in the murder. The brand is set upon him; he is shut out from contact with all creation; he has closed the avenue of sympathy with his fellow-men; as he decides that they shall be unknown to him he becomes unknown to them.[1] The brand, forbidding human vengeance ('No man may slay him'),

[1] I am reminded by this description that the isolation of Cain was in the painter's mind the retribution that follows upon the sin of selfishness.

constitutes the most terrible part of his punishment; he is driven out from all contact with created things—unseen, unacknowledged, unknown. Not only are his fellow-men unconscious of his presence, but all animate nature has cast him out: no bird or living creature acknowledges his being. For him no bird sings, no flower blooms, evil passions haunt and follow him, making discords in his ear; but all the while, one voice, as of an angel, is heard, and more and more prevails, until worn and weary nature can bear no more, and, surrendering to the Voice, he returns to Abel's altar, there to give himself up a sacrifice; and there the angel removes the curse and he dies forgiven. I should have liked to have made a sort of psychological study of it all, not only of Cain and of Abel, but of the human beings who passed by Cain during his term of isolation." Carrying on the theme in his mind during several years, he painted a second picture called the "Death of Cain," not exhibited until 1886. The Angel in this design is seen removing the curse, and to a correspondent on this subject—Mr. Edward Butler—to whom the picture had suggested a poem in blank verse, he writes:—

"*May 25th*, 1886,
"Kensington, W.

"Dear Sir—I am much gratified by your poetic illustration of my picture, 'The Death of

---

He sometimes spoke of it as the only sin that might be called "the unpardonable," because, when carried to the utmost limit, it must entail the death of love, the most vitalising of all human instincts.

GEORGE FREDERIC WATTS

Cain.' You have exactly rendered my intention, very nobly and beautifully. The picture is one of a series illustrating a sketched-out poem of my own. Cain is, in my intention, a symbol of reckless, selfish humanity (always killing his brother). I intend simply that the sacrifice is accepted. The flaming angel sweeps away the cloud which represents the brand. I am much pleased that you felt so distinctly the return to the deserted altar.—Very sincerely yours,
"G. F. WATTS.

"EDWARD BUTLER, ESQ."

In a subsequent letter Mr. Watts adds: "I identify myself and my work with no especial dogma. I think there may be as much of Cain in sitting on one's own altar, and choosing one's form of sacrifice, as in making none at all. Cain is in the grasping of riches to the hurt of others, or in indifference to others; in the building of houses unfit for dwelling in; in the polluting of streams without regret; in short, in the absence of sympathy with the weaknesses of our fellows; and there is need to return to the deserted altar of sympathy before the cloud of unhappiness and gloom that hangs over all life can be swept away."

Pictures such as these, he knew very well, could no more make an appeal to the mind of visitors to the summer exhibition than could a chapter of Isaiah read in the midst of a company at some ordinary afternoon party in modern

London; and to this want of concord was added the necessarily destructive effect upon a painting low in tone and subtle in drawing, of conflicting colours, and the dazzle of upright and level lines of new gilding. It was, however, the message which he had come to bring, and he had to give it. The sympathy of a few friends was meanwhile a solace to him, and amongst these some two or three Manchester merchants were foremost.

Mr. Richard Johnson at this time had expressed a wish to obtain from him the painting, then incomplete, which was afterwards named "She shall be called Woman." Of this Signor writes to Mr. Rickards:—

"With regard to the proposition, I hardly know what to say. In the first place, Mr. Johnson has not seen the picture, which is a large one—seven feet high—though narrow, and he can scarcely have space for it in his house; secondly, it is a perfectly naked figure, and though I hope my endeavour to render it perfectly unobjectionable on that score has not been wholly unsuccessful, still, such subjects are more fit for a gallery than a dwelling-house, and one could not expect a household that has not been brought up in familiarity with this class of work to escape being shocked.

"Thus far, you see, I am thinking of Mr. Johnson, and am anxious he should not feel like the man who came into possession of a white elephant. Now, as for what concerns myself, these designs—Eve in the glory of her innocence, Eve yielding to temptation, and Eve restored to beauty and nobility by remorse—form part of one design and can hardly be separated, any more than one would think of separating the parts of an epic poem. My intention was to make them part of an epic, and they belong to a series of six pictures illustrating the story in Genesis, viz. the three Eves—'The Creation of Eve,' 'After the Transgression,' and 'Cain'— three single figures, and three full compositions. These I always destined to be public property, and if I could afford to do so I would paint them and present them to Manchester. Such hope have I of Manchester from my knowledge of yourself, Mr. Johnson, and Mr. Barlow, all caring for art in the highest sense, and sympathising with efforts that meet with very little popular encouragement. But I don't suppose it will ever be in my power to carry out such an intention."

From this letter it is evident that the hope of having the means given to him to create the great epic of life, and story of mankind, had been entirely given up; and that the scheme which was in some measure to take its place— his gift of pictures to the nation of a certain class of subject—had been decided upon, though not their final destination. The want of general sympathy with this object was very bitter to him, though it did not embitter him. Like the young knight in "The Court of Death," he accepted with bowed head the verdict, laid down his dearest hope, and went on to work upon that which was left to him. He wrote of this, in a note perhaps only meant for his own eye: "I feel as some athletic man who, awaking from a fever, finds himself reduced to half the strength of infancy; as Samson might have felt, when shaking off his lethargy, and shorn of his locks feels the wonderment of strangeness, the despair of weakness."

He would at any rate enter into and do something to forward his friend Mr. Ruskin's lofty ideals. St. George's Guild was in the making, and he proposed to help him in this matter. "I hope you fully understand that I intend to join you in your scheme, though I am not sure it will result in any practical success. I know nothing about that, perhaps it is entirely Utopian. I don't care, it is a protest against Mammon-worship, and the giving up of everything in the desire to 'get on'—characteristics of the age I cannot but deplore. Whilst I perceive that they are natural, at least I wish to add my name to the list of those who think that humanity, and even society, is capable of better objects. The assistance I can lend you will be but very little indeed, and I offer it only as a proof of sympathy. The tenth of my earnings I will give yearly, but that will amount to very little, for my professional (labours) are not valued in the market; and, after having worked indeed very earnestly for five-and-twenty years, I have not succeeded in realising enough to give me—after satisfying just claims—if I should be from accident unable to work, £50 a year. But that need not be thought of while I can work. I do not complain, I do not know that I even feel disappointed. The fault is mine, no doubt. If I had possessed real power, I should have commanded success. The only thing that sometimes crosses my mind is that some of the many with worth and influence whom I have known, and who have professed to believe in my capacity, and in the direction of my aim, might have shown without material difficulty the material sympathy without which I have failed to carry out my aspirations."

To this letter Mr. Ruskin replies:—

"Denmark Hill,
"May 10th, 1871.

"My dear Watts—I am deeply grateful for your letter. You can, of course, help us in all the best and most noble ways. I do not move in any wise until next year, when my purpose will be completely laid before all who care to know it. I will then hope that you will consider of it deliberately before giving it the sanction of your name. I would fain have no man regret joining hand with me.— Ever affectionately yours, J. Ruskin."

During the lamentably short career as an artist of George Mason, Signor became greatly attached to him. He lent him at one time a studio at Little Holland House, and there, I think I am right in saying, the "Harvest Moon" was painted. I know he told me that he had seen that moon travel from one end of the picture to the other, and finally go back to its original place in the design. He said that there were quite six pictures on that canvas. The artist Frederick Walker was a very constant visitor at old Little Holland House, and Signor spoke of the attractive qualities of his nature. He liked to recall that when the picture "Man goeth forth to his Labour unto the Evening" came before the Hanging Committee at the Academy not one word was spoken, but a burst of spontaneous applause was given to it by every member clapping his hands. I remember one morning as we walked down the village street of Compton (Surrey), the splendid figure of a young countryman went along before us, and Signor exclaimed, "How like Walker! and yet critics objected to his ploughman because they said it was too like a Greek statue in modern clothes." He pointed out, however, that there is a possibility of a scientific arrangement of line becoming too apparent, and in the avoidance of this Jean François Millet went further than Frederick Walker.

The building of the new home at Freshwater in the Isle of Wight began in the summer of 1872. The attraction to that place was that both Farringford and Mrs. Cameron's house were in the near neighbourhood, also that the climate of the Isle of Wight was mild, and certainly in May the untouched, unbevillaed country of the Isle of Wight was a paradise of beauty. To make money for the building he set himself to the unwelcome task of painting portraits professionally, writing that it is " an occupation as distasteful to me as any exercise of my profession can be." He made engagements sometimes with three sitters in one day, the consequence being that later he was much knocked up and went to Brighton for some weeks to recruit. He was, however, unfortunate enough to have a bad kick on his shin from a horse the first day he happened to be out with the Brighton Harriers, and so was laid up for some time, the pain and confinement to his room obliging him, as he writes, to spend " much time being ill and getting well." It was here, and now, that he took upon himself the guardianship of a little orphan girl. It so happened that a young widow, a great-niece of Mrs. Prinsep's, had died quite suddenly, leaving several little children, and, being at Brighton, they were brought to see the Prinseps. They had not been very long in the room when the youngest—a tiny thing to wear so black a frock—made her way to Signor's side, found him to her liking, jumped upon his knee, and so into his heart. She came to live at Little Holland House under Mrs. Prinsep's care, but she was to be his little Blanche.

GEORGE FREDERIC WATTS

A year or two before this time the volume of poems written by Dante Gabriel Rossetti had been published. These poems placed Rossetti, in Signor's estimation, amongst the greatest of our English poets. To him the poet Rossetti stood higher than the painter.

It appears to be doubtful whether Rossetti knew, or did not know, that it was Signor's intention to paint for the National Collection the portrait for which, soon after the appearance of the poems, he was asked to give sittings, though the portrait was certainly painted with this view. It is quite possible that Signor forgot to mention its destination, or if he did mention it, that the poet had forgotten this in 1875, when he wrote asking if he might have it in exchange for a crayon drawing, unnamed, but labelled, " Drawn in Chalk by Dante G. Rossetti, 1874."

It was in fact straining generosity to breaking point, and possibly Rossetti afterwards recognised this, when he wrote his thanks for the gift.

" 16 CHEYNE WALK,
"<i>26th August</i> 1875.

" MY DEAR WATTS—You must have thought me very ungrateful in not having written again till now.

" On seeing the portrait anew, I really felt that I had asked too much of you. I remembered it only as a beginning, and had no idea that it was so happy and brilliant an example of your work, or a framed picture so near completion. In proposing the exchange I wished for it in order to make a present, having always found it impracticable to paint my own portrait. Were it not for this I must in conscience have offered it you back again, seeing the utter inequality of the exchange as it stands; but things being thus, I will instead beg your acceptance of some further memento of my work, such as it is, when I have anything worthy of you at disposal.

"I feel sincerely that I have unduly taxed your friendly feeling, and that you have responded as few would have done.

"You know how glad I should be to see you here any time, but I am well aware that you are little more given up to visits than myself. Moreover, I am not an early riser, and afternoons are of course precious with you. I will hope to see your own works one day yet.—Ever yours sincerely, D. G. ROSSETTI."

To which the reply was:—

"MY DEAR ROSSETTI—It gives me infinite pleasure to find that you like the picture. We will not bandy compliments or I might tell you how much I value your drawing. I cannot think you indebted to me and should be very unwilling to take anything more from you in return; that would be to rob you of your time and labour, a very unjustifiable sort of proceeding, though of course I should like to possess any number of your works.

"I hope you are working, and when I am settled shall make an effort to come and see you ; meantime I am obliged to you for giving me the opportunity of affording you pleasure.— Yours very sincerely,   G. F. WATTS."

A mutual friend once told him that Rossetti's reason for asking for the portrait was that a great dislike for it had so grown up in his mind that he wanted it to destroy it; but, on seeing it, he was greatly surprised to find that it was so fine a portrait. What truth there is in this story I cannot say, and the letter quoted gives a different version.

The picture, after Rossetti's death, came into the possession of Mr. Frederick Leyland ; it was said that he bought it from a pawnbroker. My husband, deeply regretting that his collection was without that portrait, got permission from Mr. Leyland to make a replica by his own hand.

Of the two paintings, Mr. William Rossetti, brother of the artist, wrote to Mr. Watts in 1892 : "Will you allow me to express my thanks to you for that very beautiful portrait of my brother ? I looked on it long with deep interest and satisfaction. It will continue to long distant years to represent my brother to his countrymen in the most advantageous light, and a truthful one too. Certainly in that

GEORGE FREDERIC WATTS

Victorian Exhibition you have made my brother shine forth pre-eminently among his contemporaries, both for aspect of genius and for those attractive qualities of person which one is glad to associate with mental superiority. I think the original exceeds (as was natural under the circumstances affecting the two cases) in the look of personal presence and activity: on the other hand, I think that the duplicate exceeds in suavity of expression, and in the sort of beauty which accompanies this, and it is not less of a definite likeness."

Not many years later, when the Leyland collection of pictures was in Christie's auction rooms, Mr. Woods was told the story of this portrait, and was asked to mention how it had strayed from Mr. Watts's possession. Perhaps in consequence of this, Mr. James Smith (of Blundell Sands) bid for the picture, and, becoming its possessor, subsequently kindly allowed Signor to exchange it for another work. And so the original picture was restored to the collection at Little Holland House, and is now in the National Portrait Gallery. At the memorial exhibition of Dante Gabriel Rossetti's paintings at Burlington House in 1883, this portrait was on an easel; and, surrounded by all the mystic poetry of Rossetti's imagination, it was found to be not less subtle or mystic, although but a literal record of a man, and so belonging also to the prose of everyday. The poet in Rossetti was what the painter wished to honour, and to the presence of a poet in this portrait he endeavoured to bring the spectator. As I (and that not seldom) read to him from "The House of Life," from "The Rose Mary," or from "Hand and Soul," he listened with ever-increasing admiration. He placed the sonnet called "Lost Days" beside the very greatest in the English language. He liked to talk of him with old and intimate friends, such as Mr. Watts-Dunton and Mr. Frederick Shields, and I can never forget the emphasis laid by the saintly Mr. Shields upon these words: "Depend upon it, Rossetti had a very holy mind." And that marvellous bit of a poet's prose, "Hand and Soul," witnesses to this.

Signor saw very little of Rossetti during these later years; his own habit of keeping within his studio walls and Rossetti's failing health led naturally to this; but there was no sort of breach between them. When Rossetti was younger, and perhaps less occupied with work, he came often to Little Holland House. Later, these visits were less frequent, and in 1868 Signor writes to him: "I have been constantly on the point of going to see you, as I am always anxious to know what you are doing, but you and I are not good at visiting." And the following year he says: "I don't ask you to come and see what I have for exhibition, I always dislike the whole thing, and am disgusted with my work; however, if you should be out this way, I need not say, 'Pray, walk up and see the gems!'" He never met Mrs. Rossetti (Miss Siddall), about whom in a postscript of a letter from Mr. Ruskin to Signor I find these lines : " Yes, Rossetti's a great great fellow, and his wife is as charming as the reflection of a golden mountain in a crystal lake, which is what she is to him."

"I wish I had seen her," Signor once said to me. " I told Rossetti that I was sorry I had not met his wife, and he answered, ' Oh, come and dine. I will write to you.'" Sometime afterwards he wrote : "I did write to ask you to dinner, but as you did not come I thought the letter had miscarried, and I was partly confirmed in that impression by finding it in my pocket."

One of the saddest stories in the annals of Art was told to Signor by Rossetti. An elderly man once came to see him, and bringing specimens of his paintings and drawings with him, had begged Rossetti to give him a candid opinion upon them as to whether they were worthless or not. Rossetti looked at them carefully, wondering how he could break to the poor man the fact that there was nothing good in them whatever, and eventually he gave him to understand this as kindly as he could. The man then drew out from under his coat another collection of drawings, and spread them out before Rossetti, telling him that they were the work of a young student. Rossetti was delighted, exclaiming that they showed remarkable talent, and that there was every reason to believe that the young student would distinguish himself. "Ah, sir," said the poor man, "I was that student." The letters from Rossetti to Signor are evidence of his wish to be of use to younger men; each one is written with the object of serving some one, and he applies to Signor to lend a helping hand.

In March 1873 the portrait of John Stuart Mill was painted. The undertaking of this was the outcome of conversations with Sir Charles Dilke, while painting his portrait and that of Lady Dilke, in the early months of the year. Mr. Mill wrote to Sir Charles: "I hardly know how to answer your very kind and flattering proposal regarding a portrait. I have hitherto disliked having my portrait taken, but I am unwilling to refuse the high compliment paid me by Mr. Watts and yourself; and if sittings can be arranged within the limited time of my stay in London, I shall be happy to make an appointment." Miss Helen Taylor, his stepdaughter, had also urged him to consent to Sir Charles's request. Of the first appointment Signor writes on March 17: "Mr. Mill is to come to-morrow to give me a sitting." As this is the only portrait for which Mr. Mill ever sat, it may be reckoned amongst the most fortunate accidents of the artist's career that he succeeded in painting what must be called one of his most subtle delineations of character.

During these sittings Mr. and Mrs. Fawcett came to see the portrait, and I think then first made acquaintance with Signor. Mrs. Fawcett tells me that Signor seized that characteristic of Mill which gave the impression of his great refinement and delicacy. I remember that my husband found himself entirely in agreement with Mr. Mill when he said that the real change required for social reformation is a change of character. He found his sitter surprisingly sympathetic; sensitive to all that was beautiful in form and poetic in thought.

Mr. Mill left for France early in April and died at Avignon on May 8. Signor was able to make a replica of the portrait for the National Collection, and was so far satisfied with this that he doubted whether the replica did not surpass the original. Sir Charles, however, preferred to purchase the original portrait, and this is now, by his bequest, the property of the City of Westminster. The duplicate is in the National Portrait Gallery. Later, Signor made yet another. It was not to be expected that the level could be sustained, and this replica—certainly in Sir Charles Dilke's opinion—lacked some of the inspiration in the other two paintings.

The picture was etched by Rajon, at Sir Charles's desire; and of this Signor writes, when he sends the original portrait and replica for inspection :—

"*August* 28*th*, 1873,
"LITTLE HOLLAND HOUSE.

"DEAR SIR CHARLES—I send you the two pictures and the photograph. I am told that it would be best to have the picture etched, and that there are some French engravers who would do it very well. I think Mr. Stephens would be able to give information on the subject. I know little or nothing about such matters.—Yours very truly, G. F. WATTS.

"*P.S.*—I believe according to law it is necessary to mention that the copyright of a picture is, or is not, disposed of with it, and in parting with my portrait of Mr. Mill I must reserve the copyright."

To Miss Helen Taylor Sir Charles very generously offered to give the picture, but she would not accept this for herself, and, writing from abroad, suggests that she should be allowed to ask Mr. Watts to make a replica for her to give to the nation, but the painter had already forestalled her wish.

He makes an allusion to the sittings, under the date of March 28, 1873, in writing to Mr. Rickards of Mr. Johnson's wish to possess the picture he afterwards called "Chaos": "Without reference to the success or failure of my work as a painting, I feel sure that Mr. Johnson will gain no small credit for the proof given of sympathy with endeavours to give utterance to the highest qualities of art, as such sympathy is very rare in England, even where it might be expected to exist.

"Yesterday I told one of our most profound

thinkers and most influential amongst our influential men (referring to yourself and Mr. Johnson) that from Manchester and commerce I had received encouragement to carry out those abstract views which he to my satisfaction was finding full of interest—I had failed to receive from those whose inherited position, whose education, wealth, and leisure, constituted the natural fosterers of the noblest aspirations in Art; he was surprised."

During these later years, both Mr. and Mrs. Prinsep were more or less invalids. The hospitality at Little Holland House could not be offered in the same liberal way, and Mr. Watts's life continued to be one of arduous devotion to work, his ride every morning for health's sake being the only interruption permitted. His companion on these rides was, more often than not, Mr. Prinsep's niece, May Prinsep, whose home from childhood had been at Little Holland House, and who now a grown-up young lady was going out in London. Old and young friends joined them, and the ride in the Park made a pleasant hour in the day of work. It was now that he saw something of Mr. and Mrs. George Lewes, and would have painted " George Eliot " for the National Collection; but he knew that the features belonged to a type he would have found most difficult; and afraid of not doing the great mind justice, he did not venture to make the attempt.

To her he writes, thanking for her appreciation of his "Clytie": "I would pay my respects to you and Mr. Lewes, but I am a wretched creature, and dare not go out in the evening, or even in the daytime, unless the weather is perfect; then every moment is required for work. But if—kindly overlooking the apparent want of respect due to you and Mr. Lewes—you would sometimes give me your opinion of things scattered about in my studio, it could not but be of great service to me. I aim at what is beyond me, and, in a wholly unsympathetic age, struggle with my half-formed conceptions; miserable in the consciousness of my incapacity. You who can not only imagine but give perfect form to your poetry, cannot fortunately realise such a struggle with phantoms." When thanking him for a cast of "Clytie" he had sent her, she tells him that she had heard from Mr. Rossetti that he had long been, and was still, suffering from bad health, and adds: "*That* experience is almost sure to include some sadness and discouragement. Therefore when I tell you that such conditions have made a large part of my history, you will understand how keenly I feel the help brought me by some proof that anything I have done has made a place for me in the mind which the world has good reason to value; and this strong proof from you happens to come at a time when I especially needed such cheering. The bust looks grander in my eyes, now that I can turn to it from time to time."

GEORGE FREDERIC WATTS

During the autumn of 1873, the new house at Freshwater was finished; but for Mr. and Mrs. Prinsep, both being somewhat of invalids, the dry air of Bournemouth was recommended, and three months were spent there; Signor also recruiting after two strenuous years in which he had been surpassing his usual record of work. He was also glad to know that his companionship was a solace and comfort to his friends.

I thought myself very fortunate at this time to be with an elder sister at Bournemouth for a week, and used to feel very shy and very proud, when Mr. Watts came to see us, and took us for a walk, or when we went to find him at Trinity Lodge. I remember his pointing out beauty in the bare branches of trees in villa gardens, or perhaps in sky or sea; but what I remember most distinctly was the sense of being in an unusual presence. This had not so much to do with anything that he said, as it had to do with that which he was. It gave me a feeling of awe, and I was always grateful for his patience, and wondered at his understanding of a girl's stupid timidity.

From Trinity Lodge he writes to Mr. Rickards, who had disappointed him by his want of appreciation of the picture "The Shadow of Death," by Holman Hunt: "With regard to the intention of the work I do not feel as you do; I think the painter more than justified in illustrating the historical side of his subject, and there is something very touching in the words, 'He was subject to his parents.' I feel also that there is much real religious poetry in the allusion to the dignity of labour, and charm in the idea conveyed of human love between Mother and Son. As to my own picture ('The Spirit of Christianity') it is wholly different, and not to be placed in the same category in any way whatever. Mine is but the symbol of compassionate tenderness. I take an idea that may be accepted by all Christian Churches, and even, I think, by the hardest philosophy which will admit the divinity of love and charity, too much forgotten, it appears to me, in all the contributions to the controversy. I have not time to write at any length, or endeavour to express myself properly. I shall look forward to showing you my picture, but I doubt if you will find it satisfactory; I don't think it can be fairly called a religious picture, certainly not a doctrinally religious picture."

The spring of 1874 found the Prinsep family settled at the Briary, while Signor arranged to remain one more year at Little Holland House. Although at the Briary he had now built two good studios, he soon realised when there how difficult it would be for him to live so far from London. Therefore his friend Mr. Frederick Cockerell was preparing plans for a new house on a piece of ground sub-let to him by Valentine Prinsep, who had found his garden, and the ground-rent he paid for this, too large. Lady Holland, burdened by the management of the property, had now made it over to her successor, Lord Ilchester; and with him, or his agent, business arrangements had to be made. All such matters troubled Signor greatly; he had not the faculty for business he so greatly admired in Leighton, and with which even the poetic mind of Dante Gabriel Rossetti seemed to have been endowed. It fretted him when he had to give up time from his work to such considerations, and much now happened to thwart and annoy him.

The work of the memorial to Lord Lothian, commissioned by Lady Lothian for the church at Blickling, and a replica for Jedburgh Abbey were in hand, as well as the Hugh Lupus for the Duke of Westminster, and he felt more or less paralysed by the thought of removing all this work to a new studio. He had also undertaken, on behalf of the Benchers, to paint a portrait of the Prince of Wales, and was anxious that the sittings should if possible be all at his own studio; but this was not found practicable, and he was under the disadvantage of having at times to take his work to Marlborough House, and so to paint in different lights; also of having to retouch without the presence of the sitter, a thing he never cared to do when painting from life. In spite of these disadvantages, the sittings left a pleasant impression. The considerate thoughtfulness of the Prince struck him much, and he formed a very high estimate of his abilities, and regretted that he had not long been given more responsible work for the country.

Old Little Holland House from the South West

GEORGE FREDERIC WATTS

There were frequent interruptions, and the portrait of the Prince was not exhibited till 1882, when it met with hostile criticism, which caused him to withdraw the picture and beg the Benchers to ask Mr. Frank Holl to paint the Prince, at the same time returning their cheque. Early in February (1875) he returned to Little Holland House, believing that he should have to leave it at Lady Day. However, so overwhelming was the task of removing and rehousing the great accumulation of work contained in four studios, that it was found to be quite impossible to arrange all in the time. He was therefore fortunate in being able to obtain a further lease of part of the old house, with his studio, now surrounded by the *débris* of the half-demolished walls, till the end of the following August. He was working hard to finish his large picture, the "Spirit of Christianity." Certain discussions between Church and Church had made him anxious to paint what to him was the Life of the Life in all religion, and this picture was shown at the summer Exhibition. It suffered much from its surroundings, seeming to him to be out of place; but he writes :—

"I do not in my more thoughtful pictures work expecting that the drift and higher qualities of my aims will be discovered or cared for, as a rule; but, though I am not influenced by this consideration, trusting to, and satisfied with, the justice of time, the sympathy of a few minds is always most encouraging, if only as proof that I am not wholly deceiving myself with regard to such aims; therefore it is a great pleasure to me to find the Bishop reading my imperfect work aright. I was surprised to find that Ruskin found something in the picture,[1] and though his praise could hardly be called very cordial, or unqualified, it was far more than I expected."

The large picture called the "Mid-day Rest" had also to be completed. Some years before (in 1863), the dray, the horses, and the carman were lent as models to Signor through the kindness of Mr. Charles Hanbury. Believing that this particularly fine breed of horses would, under the inevitable changes of time, practically disappear, he had already approached a firm of brewers, making known his wish to paint these animals, and had politely asked the firm if they could see their way to lend a pair to him for such a purpose. For answer he had received a curt refusal, with the information that the firm required no such advertisement. On hearing this Mr. Hanbury, anxious to vindicate the honour of brewers, immediately wrote to assure Signor that Messrs. Hanbury, Trueman, and Co. would be proud to send him, at any time, the finest specimen they could select of both carman and horses.

Accordingly in Little Holland House garden the picture was painted, a special arrangement of temporary roofing being set up round the

---

[1] In his criticism Mr. Ruskin admits that this picture "belongs to the inevitable expression in each period of the character of its own faith."

canvases upon which he made the necessary studies.

He had just completed the "Ariadne in Naxos," and speaks of it as the most complete picture he had ever painted. It was bought by Mr. Rickards, but became better known in London when, after his death, it came into the possession of Lord Davey, who so generously lent it to many exhibitions. A still better known design was on his easel, and had been so for some time: this was the first version of "Love and Death";[1] it had been exhibited at the Dudley Gallery in 1870, and at Manchester in 1874. On its return to his studio it was almost repainted, and completed in July of this year. He liked to send his pictures to exhibitions before their final completion, and said he did so purposely, as he thought he might learn something by seeing them placed in what he usually found to be unfavourable conditions. In Manchester the picture had been greatly cared for, some of his friends being most anxious that it should be acquired for that town by public subscription. In writing of this a friend had called it "Love Restraining Death," and he replies: "I hope it is not so called in the catalogue. Love is not restraining Death, for it cannot do so; I wish to suggest the passionate though unavailing struggle to avert the inevitable.

[1] The canvas of this first picture measures 69 inches by 29 inches, and is now in the Art Gallery of Bristol.

GEORGE FREDERIC WATTS

"You know my great desire to use such talents as I may have, and such experience in art as I have been able to acquire, with the object of proving that art, like music and poetry, may suggest the noblest and tenderest thoughts, inspiring and awakening, if only for a time, the highest sensibilities of our nature. If an individual feels, for five minutes, the best part of his nature called into activity, he has been a gainer; and in this way I hope to deserve well of my fellow human beings. Such designs as 'Love and Death' and the 'Angel of Death,' with certain others, I hope to be able to paint and present to public institutions at Manchester or elsewhere; wherever, in fact, I might feel they would best perform their mission." At this time he also writes: "I have about twelve to fifteen very large pictures which it will be a great point of conscience to paint, and I can only hope to succeed by giving up the rest of my life to them. When I get to work in my new studio I shall be better able to judge. You may be sure if I cannot undertake all you desire it will not be for want of will but want of power."

CHAPTER IX

Art is a language. The habitual use of it will create the impulse and power to express ideas and thoughts. That Art which simply says, " This is a flower," even though describing accurately enough its form and line, is inferior to the Art which, while showing these, becomes an interpretation of the poetry of Nature.

G. F. WATTS.

CHAPTER IX

SOME few years previous to this date (1875), among the large canvases standing about in the studio was one upon which had been made the sketch of a life-sized horse, with its rider, a mailed figure, standing by the bridle. The knight had been painted from the convenient model always at hand, even at 4 A.M.; and as a portrait it recalls very truly what Signor was in 1870. Despairing of ever carrying the whole design further, he now had the canvas cut down, the casque and plume of peacock's feathers were added, and the picture of the knight passed into the possession of Mr. Rickards, who named it the " Eve of Peace."

Although this picture, as a portrait, conveys the impression of a man of action, physically stronger and bigger, and therefore does not give the almost ethereal impression produced by the painter's own aspect, it is otherwise very much as he looked when I first saw him in 1870.

My people had been introduced to him in 1867. They were in London during May and

GEORGE FREDERIC WATTS

June, and Mrs. Cameron, who had been photographing my two elder sisters at Freshwater, was urgent that they should be seen by her "divine artist."

The letters describing their visit to Little Holland House are connected, in my mind, with twilight and scent of lovely May evenings in the Inverness-shire highlands. The birch in tiny leaf and the bog-myrtle we brushed through made the air sweet when, after schoolroom tea, my cousins, my younger sister and I, with our respective governesses, all set out for a walk to meet the postman, due between eight and nine in the evening. I heard that Mrs. Prinsep, though an invalid at the time, had received them with her usual generous welcome. One of my sisters sat beside her, and in her impulsive way Mrs. Prinsep called to the painter, who was present, to join in her expressions of admiration. She drew his attention to her golden hair, which she called "an aureole," much to the discomfiture of her young visitor. My sister never forgot the restrained and quiet rejoinder, which instantly set her at her ease, "I am not going to pay compliments. Young ladies do not like it."

As the next two years were, for us, chiefly spent on the Continent, there was no opportunity of being again at Little Holland House. It was therefore not till 1870 that I first went under its thatched porch, and waited in the room of the blue ceiling till summoned to the studio, to pass with a beating heart through a

GEORGE FREDERIC WATTS

red baize-covered door. There we read with some feeling of awe a large label—" I must beg not to be disturbed till after two o'clock "—before it was pushed back, to swing again heavily behind us; the studio door opened, and Signor came forward to meet us. By that date we had become intimate with the great pictures in the Dresden Gallery, going to it nearly every day for nine months. We had spent days in Venice and Florence, and a winter at Rome. Now at all modern exhibitions I acknowledged to myself that George Frederic Watts was the painter of painters for me.

In 1870 the beard was only slightly touched with grey, his hair quite brown, very fine in quality, and brushed back from the forehead. I do not recollect that I saw the picture of the knight with bowed head now called the " Eve of Peace." I remember the painter much more distinctly than his work; but he nevertheless so distinctly suggested to me the days of chivalry that I believe I should not have been surprised if, on another visit, I had found him all clad in shining armour.

From this time forward I received the greatest kindness and help from him. His patience with amateur work, his appreciation of anything that was a natural expression in any art, is so well known that nothing further need be said. I was one of the many who brought their efforts to show him, and who, coming to learn something to enable them to draw better, went away feeling they had also learnt how to live better.

But again to take up the story, five years later, from which an excursion backwards has been made.

The last entry of rent for "a part of Little Holland House" shows that it was paid up to August 31, 1875. He had then been able to build what was always known as the Iron House, or sometimes as the "Tin-pot": a studio in one corner of the new ground, where much could be stored till the studios in the new house were completed. There was provision made on the original plan for an extra studio, upon which Mr. Burne-Jones's name is written as owner; a pleasant proposition, made between the two friends, but which was never realised. Though two large canvases stood there for many years, with certain designs upon them by the hand of Sir Edward Burne-Jones, he never painted there; and the canvases were at last claimed, and the partition between the two studios, which had already been moved back some twenty feet, was finally removed altogether, and in the end only the two doors, side by side, remained to show what had been intended.

It was now that his old friend, Mrs. Charles Wylie, dismayed at the thought of the destruction of all the frescoes at Little Holland House, asked him if she might try to remove them from the walls. There was much correspondence between them, he being reluctant to allow her to undertake such a labour of love. But as she insisted he consented ; and so, with two workmen under her, she saved a great many of these.

These decorations made a sort of frieze round the room known as the upper dining-room, and were also in the corridor of the old house. They were packed in cases which naturally were very cumbersome and had to be stored for two or three years by a builder. On the death of this man, they were sent to Mr. Watts in Melbury Road. Later he gave them to Mrs. Barrington, who has preserved them on the walls of her house.

Mrs. Wylie had a considerable knowledge of the methods employed by the old masters, and possessed a fine artistic gift that, unfortunately, her parents had not allowed her to cultivate ; otherwise she would certainly have made her mark. Her married life did not leave her much opportunity for study, but a copy she made for Signor of a portion of Titian's "Bacchus and Ariadne," he liked to keep constantly before his eyes ; and Sir Frederick Burton, who, as Director of the National Gallery, had seen so many fail in their attempts to copy the picture, was amazed when he first saw this copy and considered that she had entirely mastered the quality of Titian's colour. Signor liked to have her advice, and often sought her help for the preparation of canvases ; and she sometimes laid in work for him in monochrome. She was a kind friend at the time of the removal from the old house to the new; seeing that the pictures were removed carefully, and later that they were preserved from damp; and to her he writes from the Briary, September 22, 1875:—

"I cannot come up to town as soon as I expected, being, besides other matters, again immersed in drains, which I find equally unsalubrious and expensive. I shall, however, come as soon as I can, for I greatly wish to see what has been done. I cannot thank you enough for all the trouble you have taken; do pray let me know something about the expense. I mean what it has actually cost you, for I cannot think that you have been able to avoid spending money. At least let me return this, without delay; this is most necessary to my comfort. You do not tell me anything about the extra studio, the walls of which I hope are up by this time. I am very anxious to have some detailed account."

And again, a month later, he says:—

"I have left off thanking you for the trouble you so kindly take, and have taken. I will ask you, if not inconvenient, to pay Tupper for me; if you will send me the account I will send you a cheque. There are lots of things you have paid for me; do not let me get into nasty little debts. I am so indolent about these things that I am likely to find myself in certain difficulties, if you allow me to go on forgetting.

GEORGE FREDERIC WATTS

We go on having wet weather here, and I am beginning to be very anxious about the things in the 'Tin-pot': please let me know if Conrad is taking any active steps. I told him to give you the key of the sculpture studio gallery.—Yours most sincerely, G. F. WATTS."

The saving of the frescoes having cost Mrs. Wylie so much time and labour, Signor begged her to accept them for her own studio; but she, knowing his ways, thought this was as usual the too generous return he liked to make for anything done for him, and refused to accept the gift.

While at work at the old house, where during its destruction she had to be every day, she was called to see a charred beam in the upper dining-room, and told me that a few more days of heat from the kitchen fire, and the beam must have been alight,—and the house with all its contents in danger of being burnt to the ground.

The new Little Holland House, for he transferred the name, was the first house built in the Melbury Road. Mr. Cockerell, knowing of the trouble at the Briary, took care there should be no recurrence of it here, from mistakes or carelessness on the builder's part. The work was thoroughly well done; and in November some rooms were practically ready for his use; but that autumn and winter were spent by him at the Briary.

Freshwater, even in winter, was never a

dull place. Interesting people came and went, attracted by Farringford. Then life seemed to hum like some big wheel round the Cameron household, so that it was impossible for the place to become sleepy.

One amusing Cameron episode Signor liked to tell to his friends. A drive had been arranged by Mrs. Cameron, who wished to take the Poet Laureate, Mr. Prinsep, and Signor to see a newly built house, and the view from it which she admired. However, on arrival they found the house was let to a German Count, who had no wish to be invaded by strangers. But Mrs. Cameron was not to be repulsed, she pleaded with her usual eloquence, and at last they found themselves in the presence of the Count. To him she then introduced Mr. Tennyson as "the greatest living poet," Mr. Prinsep as "our greatest Indian Legislator," and Signor as "the greatest living painter." But here the Count had had enough, and felt that he must thus protest: "I subscribe not to that opinion, also in Germany very good painters we have."

It was not uncommon for Mrs. Cameron, after taking a house by storm—camera in hand—to succeed in captivating the owners entirely, and making them life-long friends. This was the case, I believe, with the Empress Frederic, when she was Crown Princess of Germany.

Then the coming and going between the Briary and Farringford was constant. A walk down the broad green glade and up the pathway through the "careless ordered garden" being a matter of some ten minutes' time from door to door, walks over the downs with the Poet Laureate, and his son Hallam, took the place of rides; for Signor's little mare, the friend of so many years, was failing in her old age from the feet upwards. She was turned out in the paddock, and during one of her master's absences in London showed such signs of feebleness that before his return, and to avoid for him the pain of giving the distinct order for this himself, she was mercifully helped out of life. Writing to Mr. Rickards on January 24, 1876, he speaks of this loss :—

"You mention my intention of painting my old and much valued thoroughbred mare; few things have shocked and grieved me more than finding when I came here in the Autumn, her place vacant, and being told it had been found necessary to put her out of the world; a friend of twenty years, who had never in any sort of manner deceived me, or refused to make any effort I required, or failed in the attempt! Many a delightful day we have spent together, the most delightful days of my life. If I had painted her as I fully intended to do this last Autumn, I do not think I should have parted with the picture, but as it is one of the many things that might have been, there is nothing more to be said about it."

Many old friends were attracted to Freshwater at this time, and Mrs. Nassau Senior had taken a house at no great distance, her life of active work brought to a full stop by illness;—her friends could not but be aware that she was slipping gradually from them. Signor had but lately painted the portrait of her only child, her son Walter; and this note, the last of a discussion as to whether he or Miss Synnot—a friend of hers—was to have the pleasure of giving it to her, is characteristic both of the painter and of Mrs. Nassau Senior.

"Colwall Bay Cottage,
"28th July 1875.

"My dear Signor—When I told Miss Synnot that you positively refused to take any money for the portrait of Walter, she was quite unhappy. She said that she wanted to think that the most precious thing I could have was her gift to me.

"I wanted her to take back the cheque, and she would not; she said that I was to spend it in some present for you which would be of real use, or else she should never feel that she had given me Walter's picture; so I told her that £100 did not represent more than a quarter of what a portrait by you really was, in market value. So we agreed that I would give you something that would be useful, as her share of the gift; and that for all the rest I should remain in dear Signor's debt.

"I do not feel oppressed by being in your debt because I truly love you, and I know that you truly love me, and between real friends debts do not weigh heavily.

GEORGE FREDERIC WATTS

"After this explanation you will see that I cannot pretend to give anything to the Artists' orphan fund. It would not be honest. I make no money now I am ill, and I cost a good deal, and I have no right to appear to be generous when I have no money to give away. But there is an object which I have much at heart, and to which I should have given, had I been in a position to do so. I send you a prospectus of it. If you will not make use of Miss Synnot's money for anything but charity, at least use it for that, dear Signor; and if you give £10 for the People's Play Ground, I shall not feel so regretful, as I now do, that I am too ill to make money to give away. What would make me happy, and would please Miss Synnot, would be that you should draw the money, and lodge it in your banker's hands, and draw it for charities, if you won't use it for necessaries. Though the cheque has such an old date, it is quite right, for Miss Synnot desired, that whenever it was presented it should be honoured. So I enclose it, dear kind Signor, and a great many good objects will, I know, be the better for it, and I can quite feel that it is better so spent than in Persian carpets and couches and chairs, which is what I had thought of, for your new studio.

"I am dreadfully sorry that you have gone away, dear Signor, I was so pleased to think of the possibility of your coming in at any time to have a chat. But I shall be here till the middle of September, so I trust that I shall see you again.—Good-bye, dearest Signor, I am ever yours afftly., J. C. S."

In August and September of this year, as my father[1] had taken a house at Freshwater, I had the opportunity of seeing something of Signor. Later in this year I stayed at the Briary, but now I sometimes went to find him at work in the new studio, and on what were great occasions for me, he came to find me at work, trying to paint a portrait of my sister Ethel.

The Briary in its setting of great elm trees had altogether lost any look of crude newness, both from without and within. With the old furniture, and with the household gods from Little Holland House, which Mrs. Prinsep knew so well how to place, the new walls framing these had ceased to look new. Mr. Prinsep, now an invalid, was the centre of solicitude from devoted belongings. At luncheon, Mrs. Prinsep, at the head of her table, reigned over her large family party, looking like the wife of a Venetian Doge, transplanted into the nineteenth century, Mr. Prinsep seated beside her. On his other side was the beautiful young widow—their niece, Mrs. Herbert Duckworth—her hand often resting lovingly on his shoulder. Then the beautiful young wife and her husband, May and Andrew Hichens—not yet married a

[1] Charles Edward Fraser-Tytler.

year; and her sister Anne Prinsep, my particular friend of all the party, as she had often stayed with us in Scotland. And there was Signor, with a child on each side, as he could not be parcelled out to the greater number who clamoured to sit by him also. This was the group I remember round that hospitable table.

Afterwards in the big studio, with its serene sense of noble thought, one recalls the painter's light movements to and fro, always intent on work, and yet bearing so courteously with an interruption.

One afternoon in the drawing-room, as some visitors who had driven over to call rose to say good-bye, they turned to him and asked if they might see the studio. Something in the manner of asking seemed to imply politeness rather than interest, but courteously assenting, he opened the door for them to pass out, drew back behind it to hide a distinct shudder, caught my look of sympathy, and answered it half smiling, while I was uplifted with pride at being trusted with the secret of his feeling. Awake and in the studio with daylight, he was accomplishing an astonishing amount of work; three portraits were painted in one fortnight. I see him now, in my memory, looking so tired, so spiritual, but indefatigable.

Miss Ellice Hopkins writes her impressions of a visit to the Briary at this time.

"At a very unassuming looking house at the foot of the Downs lived another of the

GEORGE FREDERIC WATTS

Immortals, our great painter, who always went by the name of the 'Divine Watts.' Mrs. Cameron took us to see his studio, and to be introduced to him. We found a slightly built man with a fine head, most courteous in manner, and with the simplicity and humility of the immortal child that so often dwells at the heart of true genius. There was something pathetic to me in the occasional poise of the head, the face slightly lifted, as we see in the blind, as if in dumb beseeching to the fountain of Eternal Beauty for more power to think his thoughts after Him. There is always in his work a window left open to the infinite, the unattainable ideal."

It was now that Mr. and Mrs. Cameron's friends were astonished to hear that they were planning to exchange their home in Freshwater for one in Ceylon. Once it had been proposed there was not much hesitation or delay. Mr. Cameron longed to return to the island he had loved; and though for years he had not been outside his own garden, and, as a recluse and an invalid, was never seen by his friends but in a picturesque dressing-gown, over the blue and crimson of which his white locks flowed—he suddenly borrowed a coat from his son Hardinge, and walked down to the seashore, where he had not been for twelve years. Mrs. Cameron was as willing as her husband to embark upon a voyage that would take her where already four sons had made their homes. The striking of the tents for the Cameron household was full of characteristic unusualness—Mrs. Cameron providing for every contingency possible, to the point of unconscious humour. The house was soon in a state of turmoil, their rooms piled up with packing-cases, while telegrams poured in and out, and friends came in crowds to say their farewell. All Freshwater was wailing! rich and poor. I was not present at the last act, but heard that crowds of friends gathered at Southampton to see them off, who as they returned saw railway porters also going back from the ship-side, carrying under their arms the large white mounting boards with which her photographs were always enriched. She had said, "I have no money left, but take this instead as a remembrance," as she bestowed a fine representation of Carlyle or of the "quite divine" Madonna Mary [1]—no mean tip.

During some weeks in October and November Signor was staying in Grosvenor Street with his friends Mr. and Mrs. Charles Macnamara, laid up, and in the hands of his surgeon and doctor, Thomas Bond, for some surgical treatment. He returned in November to the Briary, to spend the winter there, in better health than he had known for some time.

The first completed version of his picture, then called "The Titans," now known as "Chaos," was being exhibited at Manchester. Of this he

---

[1] Mary Hillyer, who sat for the greater number of Mrs. Cameron's most successful photographs, her maid-servant, well remembered for her beauty, and for the entire absence of any self-consciousness.

writes to Mr. Rickards from Grosvenor Street, October 11, 1875 :—

"Many thanks for sending me the *Manchester City News*. I am sorry to see, by the remarks of the critic, that the arrangement of the exhibition seems to be less satisfactory than that of last year; it seems impossible that any real principle can be carried out in a modern exhibition.

"The bad effect of these exhibitions is evident in the remarks of the writer when speaking of my picture, 'The Titans' (not a good name). I don't quarrel with the critic for not liking the picture, indeed his notice is not unfavourable; but all criticisms upon pictures, whose aim is not immediately apparent, prove that such aims have no sort of interest in exhibition rooms; indeed they cannot interest when the expectation of the spectators is to be amused or interested at the first glance.

"When pictures formed part of the decoration of noble walls, an impressive effect would probably suggest to the intelligent spectator that some motive might exist, which, though not clear at the first glance, might be worth studying. It does not seem to occur to the critic that such might be the case in a modern work. Mr. Burne-Jones is more than right in not exhibiting, and I shall follow his example in the case of all but my lighter productions. If you come across the critic, tell him, with my compliments, not to suppose there can be no meaning in a thing because he may not perceive it at the first glance. Probably there would not be much meaning apparent to him in Beethoven's so-called Moonlight Sonata, especially on hearing it for the first or second time. I think I warned Mr. Johnson that it was not in the least likely to be in any degree intelligible, but I trust to time.

"I hope you are getting on well, I mean with regard to sight. I am still a prisoner to my room."

The reference to Mr. Rickards's eyesight is the first indication to be found in the letters that a serious calamity was to fall upon this kind and generous man, and true lover of art. The trouble proved to be cataract, and almost total blindness followed before relief came through a successful operation; meanwhile his cousin, Miss Chesworth, continued the correspondence. Vicariously through her and his friends he continued to enjoy his collection of pictures, and even to add to it.

The later autumn and winter were spent by Signor at the Briary, where he worked as hard as usual, but could also be merry with the children there. He was indeed looked upon as their property. They persuaded him to come and have romps with them, which meant much chasing and running, for he loved to see young things move about with the swiftness of birds; and that the little Blanche, now growing tall, could vault over a five-barred gate as easily as a boy, "and be a regular tomboy" when she liked, very much delighted him.

Mrs. Prinsep's grandchildren were also with her, so there was much merry distraction for him with these little people; children could always make him gay. There was a Christmas tree and a ceremony afterwards, when the tree was replanted by him. It rooted again and flourished, a matter in which he took a keen interest; and he found it alive and of good growth when he went to look for it in 1891. Trees were to him much like personal friends.

Upon the old site and garden of Little Holland House was now building, and to be built, a row of substantial houses; but, before the change took place, Mr. Rickards had thoughtfully sent a young artist to make watercolour sketches of the old house, and at Christmas he sent these as a present to Signor.[1]

By the beginning of February 1876 he had established himself at Little Holland House the second (6 Melbury Road). That Signor might be well taken care of, Mrs. Prinsep installed her own housekeeper, Emma Graver, and she and her mother at once took charge at 6 Melbury Road. For the sake of his health Mrs. Prinsep knew that food, however plain, must be well prepared, and knew also that in this matter, as well as for all the other comforts of his daily life, Signor

[1] From the copy of these made by Andrew Hichens and given to me by Mrs. Hichens, and partly from photographs, the drawings of the old house, used as illustrations in this book, have been made.

would be safe under Emma's care. From the new home he writes to Mr. Rickards :—

"I am afraid, in consequence of my various misfortunes, want of health in the autumn, the singularly bad weather all the winter, and the trouble attending upon my leaving Little Holland House, you will find very little done, a fact very grievous to me."

In the spring of this year Mr. Gladstone sat for the second time, or, indeed, began a series of sittings, extending over several years. This portrait was commissioned by Dean Liddell for Christchurch, the Dean being very anxious that Signor should be the painter. A little note to Mr. Gladstone, appointing the first sitting on May 12, 1876, runs thus :—

"Dear Mr. Gladstone—Tuesday will suit me better than Monday. I shall look forward to seeing you at twelve. New Little Holland House, in which you will find me, is about a hundred yards beyond the old place, and is the only house finished on the new road.—Yours very sincerely, G. F. Watts."

The sittings could only be given at long intervals of time, and went on till 1879. Light is thrown on the difficulty of achieving a good result by the final words of a letter from Signor in 1878 : "Postscript: Not a word to be spoken from the beginning to the end." Also from one of Mr. Gladstone's a year later, in which he says, "I think it is but fair also to promise that you shall be undistracted by my yielding to the temptations which the chance of a talk with you always offers."

Mr. Gladstone, as he said later, was sitting when the stress of work was unusually severe; the appointments therefore could only be made occasionally and with some interval between each. Then, as the artist was more than usually anxious to paint the man, body, soul, and spirit, the portrait proved to be a matter of extreme difficulty. He was dissatisfied himself, after painting two portraits; and as he found the subscribers were so also, he begged to withdraw, and Sir William Richmond painted Mr. Gladstone. No one was more appreciative of the success of this likeness than Signor himself; and he wrote warmly to congratulate the Dean, who replied: "I could not refrain from sending your most generous letter to Mr. Gladstone. He fully sympathises with me and is sorry, very sorry for the conditions that made it impossible for him to give the time you required; he adds slyly, that it was you who inveigled him into the conversations which caused so much distraction to you. To this no doubt you will plead guilty."

Oxford possesses, in the Bodleian, the portrait of Dean Stanley, of Lord Lothian, and of the Rev. Henry Coxe, librarian, all usually considered as belonging to the first rank of Mr. Watts's portraiture. In the Dining-Hall of

Christchurch, there are also the portraits of Dean Liddell and of Professor Jowett, both by his hand. He was now painting the small version of the "Court of Death" for Mr. Rickards, and it seems at this date to have been always called the "Angel of Death." Mr. Rickards had seen the large picture which was then in progress and desired to have a small replica, and this was being worked upon during many years. Meanwhile he had suggested two changes in the design; and Signor replies:—

"I will think over the introduction of the cross. Perhaps you wonder that I should have any sort of hesitation, but in these suggestive pictures such as 'Time and Death,' 'Love and Death,' and the 'Angel of Death,' I have a strong idea that they should appeal purely to human sympathies, without reference to creed or dogma of any kind. In one sense they are lowered by this view, but in another they are more universal in their appeal. I don't know whether you will quite follow me in this—I divide my painted poems into three classes; some are religious, some are purely philosophical, and some are simply poetical. I believe you will see my reasons if you think the matter well out, though they may not recommend themselves to your judgment—at least at first." And a few weeks later, replying to a remark made by Mr. Rickards, he says further of this picture:—

"The suggestion that even the germ of life is in the lap of Death, I regard as the most poetic idea in the picture, the key-note of the whole. You say it produces disagreeable impressions! This proves that the picture is not one for a drawing-room—the fastidiousness of modern taste being taken into account. It is a work of great gravity of character, and—as with a dramatic poem or an epic—it cannot be made up wholly of delightful fancies. But this being as I said before a small copy only, the original not being affected, I will emasculate the design so as to make it less complete, but more what the modern—I will not say unthinking—mind requires in art."

Needless to say, Mr. Rickards withdrew his objections, and begged Signor to paint what he felt he must paint.

During this summer he was very unwell, and his doctor ordered him to Harrogate. From want of health, life for him was always a struggle, and he often deplored the loss of time spent "in being ill and getting well; time lost, indeed," as he put it, "that never could be made up again." But now his doctor was firm, and he was, as he writes, "ordered off to Harrogate, which no doubt will be detestable." "Blanche and a young lady, May's sister, go with me, and will make it as pleasant as circumstances permit. I hope to be away a very short time and get to work with renewed vigour. This going to a watering-place is very hateful to me, but there is no help for it. I do not know whether or not Blanche has sent the verses on the late Little Holland House, suggested to Mr. Prinsep by the pictures you have so kindly given me; she shall write to you from Harrogate."

CHAPTER X

I HAVE done little more than desire the good thing, and seek to know nothing about the mysteries of our being, but I like to think that even unuttered aspirations may have a material force.

G. F. WATTS.

CHAPTER X

On Signor's return he found that Mrs. Tennant and her daughters were at Freshwater, and Dorothy and Evelene[1] soon became to him especial friends. They were constantly at the Briary, and he painted them there and in London, where the portraits were finished. "When Evelene sits to you again," her sister wrote to Signor, "I have a most delightful book to read to you."

Miss Tennant was working seriously at art, and wrote when she heard he was returning to the Briary for the winter: "I am so afraid of relapsing into what I was before I knew you, and seeing you once in the week even made me work doubly hard afterwards." To her persuasions in no small measure was due the writing of his first article in the *Nineteenth Century*, to which he gave as title "The Present Conditions of Art." In many letters she had urged him to write out "what would be so valuable to future and present art." One day she brought her friend M. Coquelin

[1] Who later became Lady Stanley and Mrs. F. W. Myers.

to see him, and he afterwards spent some time with her in the gallery; and she wrote later to Signor, to describe the great actor's views on art. After mentioning Coquelin's admiration for certain portraits, landscapes, and for the " Love and Death," she says : " In common with his nation he can only be appealed to—can only be touched—by reality in what he has seen, rather than what he may have felt, and he vehemently protests against art being an expression of very elevated and abstract thought. He thinks that you should stand before a picture, and that it should tell you the clearest, simplest story, and that it should appeal to you by its style and execution—by its being *masterly*. That Velasquez, Rembrandt, Holbein, Titian did not stir you by the subject or by the ideas embodied in the painting, but because they were supreme masters of pencil, brush-effects, and composition. These, dear Signor, are what I gather to be the views of French artists, and though not altogether ours, are, as you say, interesting to know." To which Signor replies :—

"*Tuesday*, L. H. H.,
"1880.

"Thanks, dear Dolly, for your letter; it tells me what I wanted to know, and I confess it impresses me with a mournful feeling to find, what I thought was true, that the brilliant and acute French intellect regards the art of painting and sculpture as a thing of passing interest—as embroidery on the intellectual needs and yearnings of our nature. Of course, its appeal being through the medium of the eye, the eye should be satisfied with the beauty of form and colour and execution—and this would be enough for what I call the passing interest; but a great picture should be a thing to live with, to respond to varying moods, and especially should have the power to awaken the highest of our subtle mental and intellectual sensibilities. To my mind it is nearer in its operation, on these sensibilities, to music than to anything else; but it must not only have the power to touch and awaken, it must have also the power to sustain the awakened and elevated spirit in that pure atmosphere that we only breathe in our happiest and least earthly moments. This can never be achieved by technical merits alone, never except by the artist throwing his whole and best self into his work. Such work may say little to the hasty observer, and the hasty observer is the ordinary amateur of art. But the few who linger to take in something more, in the course of time become a many—it is to such I would speak—but I am scribbling a lot at random, and have not time to put my thoughts into definite shapes, and these into still more definite words, but we will talk the matter over when I come to see you.—Always most affectionately yours,   SIGNOR."

The editor of the *Nineteenth Century* now

added his entreaties to those made by Miss Tennant to Signor. It was she who suggested to Mr. Knowles that such an article would be in place in the *Nineteenth Century*. He was delighted with the suggestion, and immediately acted upon it, and during the summer of 1879 the article on the " Present Conditions of Art " was written. There was, however, the inevitable delay in revising proofs, and because of the hesitation Signor felt as to its worthiness; and Mr. Knowles writes on December 16, 1879: " I am anxiously awaiting the final return of your finally corrected proof, with your final changes." The paper appeared in the February number, and Miss Tennant was satisfied, and writes to him : " I do so want to see you again, I have so much to talk to you about. I always felt certain that if you took to writing you would do much good, and surprise the public who think that a painter cannot be anything but a painter. Your article in the *Nineteenth Century* has created a great sensation. Perhaps you heard what Mr. Lowe said, that it was the finest piece of English he had read in these times. I do hope, dear Signor, you are well and vigorous. With you, the only thing wanting is a full consciousness of worth, a realising of what you are, and what you have done for others. Now, will you not write upon your theory of curves?"

The theory of curves, that Miss Tennant asks him to write about, he liked to demonstrate by pointing out the bounding line of Greek form either upon the cast of the Theseus or that of the Ilissus, both of which always stood upon the mantelpiece of his studio. Every part of the outline of these figures he saw to be fractions of very vast circles. In the flatness of the curving outline of these Pheidian sculptures he therefore perceived a suggestion of immensity. If, in other sculptures, the development of muscle was emphasised by a certain roundness intended to be impressive, he perceived that on the contrary the form became less majestic, the curve being part of a circle on a very much smaller scale. "The circle," he wrote, "is the only perfect form, equal in all its parts and complete. All lines bounding any form whatever will, if absolutely followed to the end, resolve themselves into circles; hence it will result that the impression of magnitude in complex forms (the human form for example) will depend upon the sweep of the line composing the parts of the form. Lines with a visible sweep suggest vitality, movement, and direction. Circles imply centres. All creation is full of circles which resolve into each other. The divine Intelligence must be the centre of all."

"As a principle of form in nature," he continued, "all lines curve towards their object. This is a very important fact, and must be borne in mind in the study of the human figure. Knowledge of that kind becomes a plan of construction in which everything takes its proper place without difficulty."

GEORGE FREDERIC WATTS

The decoration of the Town Hall of Manchester was now under consideration, and some of his admirers were anxious that he should undertake to fill the spaces left for fresco; but his health would not permit, and he had in hand the colossal statue upon which he was at work with hammer and chisel throughout all the fine days in summer. Then fifteen big canvases were being worked upon, and the truth that the natural limits of time were closing around him was ever present to his mind.

"If I were younger," he writes, "I should not hesitate a moment, the more especially as I think mural decoration ought to be painted *in situ*, but my health is unsatisfactory, and I have my hands full, as you know, of large subjects, and certainly I did not contemplate moving from my studio. Still, if the matter took the shape of a duty—if I thought I could aid the cause of art—I should not consider I had a right to refuse from any consideration short of necessity, health, or something of the kind. With regard to material, waterglass I do not like, or think successful; the wax process I am not acquainted with, but it is probable that it could be well adapted."

Such opportunity as this afforded should have been his many years before; it came too late now, and he could not seriously consider undertaking so huge a work, but he talked the matter over with Mr. Alfred Waterhouse—the architect of the Town Hall.

GEORGE FREDERIC WATTS

He allowed his mind to exercise itself on an arrangement of designs—an assemblage of symbolic pictures—to show the happiness that might result if the higher human aspirations could be realised ; and beside these the degradation consequent upon disobedience to divine laws. "Time, Death, and Judgment," and the "Court of Death" were to have had their place in this scheme, and also—a subject conceived yet never designed—of Adam and Eve in Paradise, surrounded by angels, symbols of those virtues which would make human conditions perfect, and constitute happiness. It was but an afterglow from his former hope that soon faded into grey reality again ; and some months later, when the work had been placed in the hands of Ford Maddox Brown, Signor wrote : "Manchester seems to be inspired with great ideas just now. I saw in one of the papers a project on the *tapis*, to connect the town with the sea, by means of a canal. This would be an undertaking worthy of a great town and, I should think, be of prodigious importance. If the rich men of all classes in England would combine to do great things, as far as great things may be done with money, instead of having for object the unworthy one of dying rich, how much better for their fame and the real greatness of the country."

During the winter Mrs. Nassau Senior had been much with her mother (Mrs. Hughes) at the house she had taken for her daughter at Colwell Bay ; and the intercourse was constant between her and the households at the Briary and Farringford. For many years her brother, a widower with four children, had lived with her and her husband and son. She adored children and undertook this extra care with joy; and now for nearly a year one of the nephews, Gerard Hughes, who had shown considerable talent for art, had been coming to draw under Signor's guidance. The first letter referring to this is of interest, as it shows how little his general view upon a student's first practice of art had changed in the many years between this date and the time when Mr. Roddam Stanhope was first at work with him.

"MY DEAR JEANIE—I send you back little Gerard's drawing; it is most interesting as displaying qualities of eye and hand, which may develop into a Fred Walker. Nothing is wanting but that knowledge which practice and study can supply. I shall be most happy to give all the aid in my power. He has been drawing here for an hour, or an hour and a half, these last two or three days. Though I am not able to be in the studio, I think the kind of work I have set him to do will exercise his eyes, hand, and judgment. It is drawing bits of drapery. Every variety of line and angle will be found in a crumpled bit of cloth, and studied upon the principles I gave you an idea of, form, I think, the best means of education of eye and hand that can be found; not so interesting perhaps as drawing the human figure, but that will come, perhaps, in a little time. I thought the casts I alluded to belonged to you; all my things in London are now in such confusion that I don't know what I have; but for the moment nothing more is necessary than what we have at hand. Do not let the boy's general education be neglected. I am confident that with judicious teaching his artistic studies for the moment need not have more than an hour or an hour and a half devoted to them. What I set him to do requires very great and fatiguing attention, and had better not be continued too long at a time. Of course as he goes on he will be able to give more time to the study, and if his father likes, the boy can come and be in my studio altogether, giving me what assistance he can in return for teaching, after the manner of the ancient practice. But this is an idea for the future. I am sorry you should take any trouble about the Sonata, it would be so easy for me to send for it. You do not say anything about yourself; is that a good or a bad sign ?—Yours affectionately,

"Signor."

In one of the last letters that passed between the two friends on this subject, he says : "You must not talk about wonderful kindness with regard to Gerard; all I can do is to go in two or three times, in the course of the morning, and look over his work, find fault, and explain some principles. As he is working in the next room to me, this is not a very wonderful exercise of generosity."

Mrs. Nassau Senior left Colwell early in February of this year (1877), believing she had made great way towards recovery; but these hopes were not to be realised. Shortly after her return home she had a serious relapse from which she did not rally, and she died on March 24.

Of this great loss he writes to Mr. Rickards without any over-estimation of what that loss proved to be to him during the nearly thirty years of life that remained for him. "I have lost a friend who could never be replaced," are his words, "even if I had a long life before me; one in whom I had unbounded confidence, never shaken in the course of a friendship very rare during twenty-six years—Mrs. Nassau Senior, who I daresay you will remember talking about with me. She had been called by a friend of yours 'that woman.'[1] I think when you read the biography of 'that woman'—for it is one that will be written—that very few canonised saints so well deserved such glorification. For all that makes human nature admirable, lovable, and estimable, she had very few equals indeed,

[1] For the reason that from 1873 she had held the post of Inspector of Workhouses, the first woman to be appointed by Government to such a position. Her special charge was to ascertain the condition of women, children, and infants in the workhouse. She worked with a zeal that was worthy of a great nature, paying visits in the earliest hours of the morning to see if the children slept in well-ventilated rooms. The prejudiced mind thought that by accepting this post Mrs. Nassau Senior had degraded her sex.

and I am certain no superiors ; and it is not too much to say that children yet unborn will have cause to rue this comparatively early death."

The summer of 1877 had, for people who loved art, an event which few can fail to look back upon otherwise than as a landmark, an event they are glad that Memory keeps fresh for them—in May this year the doors of the Grosvenor Gallery stood open for the first time. The public—not of the number of Sir Coutts and Lady Lindsay's invited acquaintance at special times, for this was their private venture—paid its shilling at the top of a broad flight of stairs, and there found the first and largest of the galleries. This room, well proportioned and well lit, had on the walls—with spaces of background restfully dividing group from group—a series of modern pictures never before so seen.

The individual taste and thought evident all about gave the pleasant sense of its being a privilege to be there. That was the first sensation. Afterwards came the consciousness that the work of some English painters of the day was being revealed to the public for the first time. And why? Because in the setting of this well-conceived building each was being allowed to deliver his message consecutively, and the visitor was not called upon to listen to him between other and conflicting voices, or to hear from him nothing but a broken sentence. The works of each artist, grouped together and divided by blank spaces, allowed the spectator's eye and mind to be absorbed entirely by what that painter had to give them; consequently this message was both understood and remembered.

Though indisputably the painter whose pictures made the chief interest of this exhibition was Edward Burne-Jones, those who had cared to search the Academy walls, season after season, for the work of George Frederic Watts, usually to find a portrait here and a portrait there, stood before the end of the West Gallery wall, and hailed their master as made known now for the first time to a larger public. For them "Love and Death" dominated the whole room. For some, through the door of their house of life the grey messenger had but lately passed; to the door of the home of some that figure was drawing very near; and as such personal response to the chord he had struck came to be known to Signor, as it did sooner or later, he felt he had not failed in the aim of his life. It was not too much to say that now to a larger public, beyond the circle of his friends, the mind of the painter was speaking for the first time, going into the intimate, into the most sacred hours of life.

After 1877, it was common for him to receive letters from strangers, some of these giving neither signature nor address, but thanking the painter with the sort of thanks he liked best to receive, for the transformation made—generally at the darkest hour of life—

through some thought suggested by one of his pictures.

With the question of the tone of the crimson damask upon the walls, and the enrichment of other parts of the gallery, which met with such severe criticism from Mr. Ruskin, Signor did not greatly concern himself. He believed that the background for rich and low-toned pictures could hardly be too strong in colour, and he preferred a rich crimson to any other; he had also long held an opposite opinion to Mr. Ruskin in the matter of seeing the work by each man kept together as much as possible.

The three portraits that Sir Coutts chose to exhibit as examples of Signor's work were the portrait of Lady (Coutts) Lindsay, of Mr. Burne-Jones, and of Mrs. Percy Wyndham, and in his letter of thanks to her he says:—

"A thousand thanks for so liberally lending me the picture. I do not know that I should have asked for it of my own suggestion, for, as you know, I am not fond of exhibiting at all; but the picture is certainly one of the best, and I hope it will look well for the sake of my friends more than my own. I have always regretted having finished it, for if it had still been on my hands, I should most likely have seen you, which now it seems I never do; but not the less you will believe that your friendship is very precious to me."

To this friend (who never failed him) he also writes: "I have so few pleasures that I can ill afford to lose the best of all—the friendship of some people."

Of the exhibition he had written a forecast to Mr. Rickards: "I think the exhibition will be a great success. Burne-Jones will be very strong, and when you have seen his works I do not think you will care much for mine. In fact I expect him to extinguish almost all the painters of the day, so you may prepare yourself for being knocked off your legs. The pictures go in to-morrow." He had written, in replying to an inquiry from Mr. Rickards: "I know nothing about the arrangements, nor have I had anything whatever to do with the enterprise, though you seem to give me credit for having been a power in the matter."

That summer at his new home in Melbury Road he was chiefly at work upon the new "Hugh Lupus"; and he writes to a friend:—

"You are quite right, I am working too hard, and could not continue to do so, but the decline of the year necessarily shortens my working time. I am now no longer able to get to work at four, but I am obliged to work all the available hours; nor must you suppose I do not put all possible concentration into each. I do not look forward to a future of repose, for I do not desire an existence when power of work is gone! But no one ought to grumble at work, even if less interesting than the pursuit of art; I do not believe in any real enjoyment outside work, or interest belonging to it."

Signor spent that winter at the Briary. Mr. Prinsep's health was giving some anxiety, and though on the whole unchanged—certainly in vigour of mind — there are evidences in the letters that he was often laid up. His son Val was in India, painting the picture of the great Durbar held by Lord Lytton on the Imperial Proclamation, naturally a visit in which the father was greatly interested. Val returned in January, but not long after his arrival Mr. Prinsep became seriously ill, and on February 11 he died. "A man of very heroic character, and extraordinary gifts and acquirements," as Signor—his friend and companion of nearly thirty years—wrote at the time of this great loss. He had with much certainty believed that Mr. Prinsep's grand physique would insure for him a great age, and many years in the peace-surrounded home he had purposely and at considerable sacrifice made for him. And that "Sweet-Briary"—as Miss Mary Boyle dubbed it — in the inevitable changes that followed Mr. Prinsep's death, practically ceased to be a home for Mrs. Prinsep, or for Signor himself, was somewhat pathetic. But life to him was a trust not to be wasted in morbid grief; the more he suffered, the more earnestly did he set his hand to his work. He was more or less laid up for a month after Mr. Prinsep's death, but he managed to finish the large picture of "Time, Death, and Judgment," for exhibition at the Grosvenor Gallery, where it was shown with "Mischief," "Ophelia," and the small "Sir Galahad," "Britomart" and five portraits being in the Academy.

In August he reports to Mr. Rickards : "I have nothing to tell you about myself. I have, as you know, a number of compositions on hand, old acquaintances of yours, which I am bringing on at the same time. This I think the best plan; I have nothing finished to show, but I insure a certain amount of completion in several important cases, and it also enables me to work longer, the change from one to another being a kind of relaxation. All the summer I have steadily used up all the daylight, and to tell the truth am beginning to feel a little tired; but I hope to hold out for another month, and then change my quarters, carrying some work to Brighton. In spite of all my labour, autumn finds me with much less done than I anticipated. My great equestrian statue is apparently not advanced; the difficulty of making every point of view equally good has necessitated constant attention; but it had better not be done at all than done in an unsatisfactory manner that the world does not want.

"I have sent some pictures to Manchester, but I really do not know what. When the pictures came out of the Royal Academy and Grosvenor Gallery, having been applied to by agents from Manchester, Liverpool, Leeds, and other places—really having no time to spare—I left the matter almost entirely in the hands of

Mr. Smith;[1] the consequence is that a letter has come to me from Leeds asking if I would sell the picture there, and I have no idea what it is."

The building in Melbury Road went on during 1876-77. Mr. Thornycroft built his two houses under one roof on one side of Little Holland House which was afterwards numbered 6 in the road, and Mr. Marcus Stone on the other side. It became, what Mrs. Thornycroft liked to call it, " Melbury Village "; detached houses, mostly built from good designs, standing in gardens of some size.

It was now that Mr. and Mrs. Barrington came to live in the next house to Little Holland House, and for some years were very constant visitors there.

I met Mrs. Barrington for the first time very shortly before our marriage. I never saw her after September 1890. She and I never really knew each other. I have this winter (1911-1912) for the first time seen and read her published recollections of my husband, and have thus been made aware that she did not really know him.

A house at Brighton had been decided upon by Mrs. Prinsep, as it suited in many ways better than the Isle of Wight. Her son Val could so easily run down to her from London; and the dryness and brightness of the winter climate she thought would be better for Signor, who was

[1] The head of the firm of carvers and gilders (who were also fine art agents), and who gave Signor service for sixty years.

likely to spend many of the shorter days away from London. It also solved difficulties of education for Blanche and the three grandchildren, now entirely with Mrs. Prinsep; therefore, by the autumn of 1876, she had settled at 24 Lewes Crescent, and a room suitable as a studio was prepared.

The change from Kensington to Brighton proved to be what Signor liked. He was always the boon companion of the young people. Blanche, now growing into a tall graceful girl, was to his great delight still quite a child; and it was a happiness to him to feel how entirely she and the little Laura and Rachel[1] gave him their confidence. They told him of their little sorrows, as well as of their pleasures; and he was often able to steer the small craft through troubled waters. Once from the group of children about him the little Laura looked up suddenly to say, "Aren't we happy chaps?"—a little saying that later Signor would sometimes quote, and one that it was always good to hear.

[1] Afterwards Lady Troubridge and Countess of Dudley.

END OF VOL. I

Printed by R. & R. CLARK, LIMITED, *Edinburgh.*

A SELECTION OF WORKS ON ART

MEMORIALS OF EDWARD BURNE-JONES. By G. B.-J. With 41 Photogravure Plates and other Illustrations. Second Edition. Two vols. 8vo. 30s. net. Cheaper Edition. With 2 Photogravure Plates and other Illustrations. Two vols. 8vo. 5s. net.

THE HERKOMERS. Vol. I. Library Edition. With 6 Illustrations. 8vo. 7s. 6d. net. Large Paper Edition. With 28 Illustrations. 4to. 25s. net. Vol. II. With 8 Illustrations. 8vo. 7s. 6d. net.

THE TRAINING OF THE MEMORY IN ART AND THE EDUCATION OF THE ARTIST. By LECOQ DE BOISBAUDRAN. Translated by L. D. LUARD. With an Introduction by Prof. SELWYN IMAGE, M.A. Illustrated. 8vo. 6s. net.

THE PRACTICE OF WATER COLOUR PAINTING. Illustrated by the work of Modern Artists. By A. L. BALDRY. With 37 Illustrations in Colour by distinguished Artists. Crown 4to. 12s. net.

THE VENETIAN SCHOOL OF PAINTING. By EVELYN MARCH PHILLIPPS. Illustrated. 8vo. 7s. 6d. net.

INDIVIDUALITY AND ART. By HERBERT E. A. FURST. Illustrated. Extra Crown 8vo. 3s. 6d. net.

MORNINGS WITH MASTERS OF ART. By H. H. POWERS, Ph.D. Illustrated. 8vo. 8s. 6d. net.

ALBRECHT DÜRER. His Life, and a Selection of his Works, with Explanatory Comments by Dr. FRIEDRICH NÜCHTER. Translated by LUCY D. WILLIAMS. With 54 Plates (1 in Colour). Imperial 4to. 6s. net.

A POPULAR HANDBOOK TO THE NATIONAL GALLERY. Including Notes collected from the Works of Mr. RUSKIN. By Sir EDWARD T. COOK. Revised and Rearranged throughout. In Two Vols. Crown 8vo. Thin Paper. Leather Binding.

    Vol. I. FOREIGN SCHOOLS. Eighth Edition. 10s. net.
    Vol. II. BRITISH SCHOOLS (including the Tate Gallery). Seventh Edition. 10s. net.

MACMILLAN AND CO., LTD., LONDON.

A SELECTION OF WORKS ON ART

THE SACRED SHRINE. A Study of the Poetry and Art of the Catholic Church. By YRJÖ HIRN. 8vo. 14s. net.

THE ORIGINS OF ART. A Psychological and Sociological Inquiry. By YRJÖ HIRN. 8vo. 10s. net.

AESTHETIC AS SCIENCE OF EXPRESSION AND GENERAL LINGUISTIC. Translated from the Italian of BENEDETTO CROCE by DOUGLAS AINSLIE, B.A. 8vo. 10s. net.

THOUGHTS ABOUT ART. By PHILIP GILBERT HAMERTON. Crown 8vo. 8s. 6d.

THE RENAISSANCE: STUDIES IN ART AND POETRY. By WALTER PATER, M.A. 8vo. 7s. 6d. net. Cheap Edition. Globe 8vo. 1s. net.

STUDIES IN THE ART ANATOMY OF ANIMALS. Designed for the use of Sculptors, Painters, Illustrators, Naturalists, and Taxidermists. By ERNEST THOMPSON SETON. Illustrated. 4to. 30s. net.

THE FRENCH PASTELLISTS OF THE EIGHTEENTH CENTURY. By HALDANE MACFALL. Edited by T. LEMAN HARE. With 40 Plates in Colour and 12 in Black. Demy 4to. 42s. net.

FRENCH PRINTS OF THE EIGHTEENTH CENTURY. By RALPH NEVILL. Illustrated. 8vo. 15s. net.

EIGHTEENTH CENTURY COLOUR PRINTS. By JULIA FRANKAU. Second Edition. 8vo. 7s. 6d. net.

A CATALOGUE RAISONNÉ OF THE WORKS OF THE MOST EMINENT DUTCH PAINTERS OF THE SEVENTEENTH CENTURY. Based on the Work of JOHN SMITH, by C. HOFSTEDE DE GROOT. Translated and Edited by EDWARD G. HAWKE. In Ten Vols. Royal 8vo. 25s. net each.

    Vol. I. Jan Steen, Gabriel Metsu, Gerard Dou, Pieter de Hooch, Carel Fabritius, Johannes Vermeer.
    Vol. II. The Works of Aelbert Cuyp and Philips Wouwerman.
    Vol. III. Frans Hals, Adriaen van Ostade, Isack van Ostade, and Adriaen Brouwer.
    Vol. IV. Jacob van Ruisdael, Meindert Hobbema, Adriaen van de Velde, and Paulus Potter.
    Vol. V. Gerard ter Borch, Caspar Netscher, Pieter van Slingeland, Gottfried Schalken, Eglan Hendrik van der Neer.
    Vol. VI. Rembrandt, Nicolaes Maes.   [*In the Press.*

MACMILLAN AND CO., LTD., LONDON.